RETURN TO THE HIDING PLACE

HANS POLEY

LIFEJOURNEY
BOOKS

ACKNOWLEDGEMENTS
The events told in the chapters "While Angels Slept" and "In the Shadow of His Wings" are firsthand accounts of those involved. For permission to use these accounts I am deeply grateful to Peter van Woerden, Henk van Riessen, Reinoud Siertsema and Simon Willemse. The translation of part of a stanza of the Dutch national hymn, *Wilhelmus*, has been quoted from the rendition in *Coming After*, an anthology of poetry from the Low Countries, by A.J. Barnouw. Published by Rutgers University Press, New Brunswick, NJ, the translation was received by the good offices of Professor Henrietta ten Harmsel.

Unless otherwise specified, Scripture quotations are from the *Holy Bible: New International Version* ©1973, 1978, 1984 by International Bible Society. Used by permission of Zondervan Bible Publishers.

LifeJourney Books™ is an imprint of Chariot Family Publishing, a div. of David C. Cook Publishing Co.
David C. Cook Publishing Co., Elgin, Illinois 60120
David C. Cook Publishing Co., Weston, Ontario
Nova Distribution Ltd., Newton Abbot, England

RETURN TO THE HIDING PLACE
©1993 by Hans Poley

Cover design by Koechel/Peterson & Associates
Interior Design by Glass House Graphics
Edited by Ron Wilson

First Printing, 1993
Printed in the United States of America
97 96 95 94 93 5 4 3 2 1

CIP Applied for.
ISBN 0-78140-932-2

CONTENTS

But the souls of the righteous are in the hand of God. . .
In the view of the foolish they seemed to be dead
      and their passing away was thought an affliction
      and their going forth from us utter destruction.
But they are in peace. . . .
Chastised a little, they shall be greatly blessed
      because God tried them and found them worthy of
      Himself.
As gold in the furnace He proved them
      and as sacrificial offerings He took them to Himself.
On the day when God deals with their case they will shine.
They shall judge nations and rule over peoples
      and the Lord shall be their King forever . . .

                                    Attributed to Solomon

To Miesje,
My Lifelong Sweetheart;
To Eusi,
My Lifelong *Chawwer**

Trusted Friend

THE TEN BOOM FAMILY

Casper ten Boom — The father of Betsie, Willem, Nollie, and Corrie, and the head of the household. Everyone except his children called him "Opa," the Dutch pet name for "grandfather."

Betsie ten Boom — The oldest child, her real name was Elizabeth, but everyone called her Bep.

Willem ten Boom — The only son, he was a minister in the Reformed Church of Hilversum. He was married to Tine, and they had several children, the eldest of whom was Kik.

Nollie ten Boom — Nollie, the second daughter, married Flip van Woerden, the principal of the Dreefschool (elementary and high school). They had three sons: Fred, Casper, and Peter; and three daughters: Aty, Cockie, and Elsjke.

Corrie ten Boom — Corrie, whose proper name was "Cornelia," was the youngest. She was nicknamed "Kees," a boy's name, because of her tomboy nature, and she became the first female watchmaker in the Netherlands.

Aty van Woerden — Aty was engaged to be married to Piet Hartog who was arrested and executed by the Gestapo for his part in the resistance.

Peter van Woerden — Peter was a talented pianist who spent many Sunday evenings playing at the ten Boom home.

Cockie van Woerden — Cockie also often visited her grandfather and aunts.

The book *The Hiding Place*, and the movie by the same name, told the story of a Dutch family, the ten Booms, and their stand against Nazi oppression during World War II. The old watchmaker and his two daughters sheltered many Jews and Gentiles who were forced to hide, but they were finally arrested by the Gestapo in February, 1944. Only daughter Corrie survived.

I was the first one to be sheltered by the ten Boom family. I lived with them and their other "guests" through eight months of tension, fear, and hope, and worked from their home for the resistance until my arrest on February 5, 1944.

Hearing of my involvement with the family and of

my life underground, many friends have asked me to write my personal story of those eventful months, but the prospect did not attract me. It would mean reliving the tension and the terror of those years. Moreover, tens of thousands of Dutch men and women could tell similar stories of their own small war. Many could relate comparable experiences or more daring activities or much deeper agonies. But the requests kept coming, so finally I gave in. With the aid of my diary which had survived the war in its own hiding place, I went back almost fifty years. I also had sixty pages of letters which I had written from hiding to Mies, my lifelong sweetheart. Private documents, plus a series of photographs I took to give her an impression of life underground, recreated wartime Holland vividly in my mind. This book, then, is an attempt to evoke, as closely to reality as possible, what happened in "the hiding place" and why.

Of course the account is subjective. It is history as I experienced it, but no less real for that.

I would not have been able to write it but for the continuing support and comment of my sweetheart, who was willing to relive with me those fateful years of our lives.

It is also a tribute to Grandfather ten Boom, his family, and many friends, who paid the highest price for their faith and obedience to God.

"Greater love has no one than this, that he lay down his life for his friends." May their memory and their example be a blessing to many.

— Wassenaar, The Netherlands
Orange City, Florida

GATHERING STORM

1

In May, 1943, the Nazis still exercised iron rule over the occupied countries of Europe. But the war was turning against them and their armies were slowly retreating. At first the Germans had tried a friendly approach to occupation, but that spring the Nazis began to show their true nature. The Gestapo intensified its merciless control, assisted by collaborating members of the Dutch *Nationaal Socialistische Beweging,* (the National Socialist Movement) traitors whom we hated like the plague. In 1941 the Nazis had set the Jewish citizens of the Netherlands apart by marking their personal identification cards with a large black "J." Later they required Jews to wear a yellow Star of David on their coats. Next they gradually restricted Jewish mobility by posting, *Voor Joden Verboden* (for Jews forbidden) signs in many places. Grudgingly the Dutch accepted these insults and restrictions. With their Calvinistic and democratic traditions, they couldn't believe that atrocities such as the German pogroms during and after the *Kristallnacht* in November, 1938, could happen within their very borders. Protests and warnings were scattered and few. We simply could not imagine the diabolical ruthlessness of Nazism.

But in 1942 and in early 1943, Gestapo raids on the Jewish quarter in Amsterdam, and the arrests of individual Jewish members of other Dutch communities, followed each other quickly. No organization existed yet to shelter and hide these people, so hundreds were rounded up, often at gunpoint, and transported to the concentration camp in Westerbork in the province of Drente. From there the trains departed with deadly regularity, carrying thousands towards the East and an unknown future—if any future at all. Hardly anyone knew then that Westerbork would become the gateway to hell. Of the Jewish Dutch community with its estimated 115,000 members, only some 8,500 survived the holocaust.

As the tide of the war turned, many non-Jews were also arrested and sent to work in the German war industry. German workers were sent to the battlefields, and thousands of young men from the occupied countries were commandeered to replace them. Soon every man between eighteen and thirty still walking the Dutch streets needed an *Ausweis,* a certificate proving to German patrols that the authorities had exempted him. Such an exemption was difficult to get; only specific groups considered necessary for

10

support of daily life qualified. Finally, at the end of April, 1943, the Germans ordered the mass deportation of Dutch students and former army soldiers and officers.

I was caught in the maelstrom because I was a student. In the summer of 1942, at eighteen years old, I had passed my university admission exam at a Christian high school in Haarlem. My parents had settled in this old Dutch city after their return in 1937 from the Dutch East Indies, where my younger brother and I were born.

My age group was still exempt from conscription for German labor, and there was nothing to keep me from starting my university studies. Almost from the beginning of the occupation, however, students had been a restive group. In November, 1940, the Germans outlawed teaching by Jewish professors at all Dutch universities. Delft Technological University, where I had been admitted, was the first to react. Students gathered to demonstrate at the class of one of their Jewish professors. Frans van Hasselt, a leader of a student fraternity, voiced the common outrage in an improvised address: "Blessed are those who are persecuted for righteousness' sake." It had an immediate effect of uniting the otherwise individualistic students around a common goal: to resist the persecutors. The students dispersed, boycotting courses and classes for the time being. Similar demonstrations were held at other universities. The Germans reacted swiftly with nationwide raids on universities. Professors and students were arrested. Delft University was temporarily closed.

In April, 1941, Delft was allowed to start courses again. When I arrived in September, 1942, everything seemed normal. But I soon learned that this was only superficial. The situation was quite tense and the students felt it.

In early December word got around that the Germans were ready again for raids and mass arrests on universities. Probably to avoid problems, Delft announced an early start of the Christmas holidays, "due to shortage of coal for heating." But I was sure that the war against the Dutch students was on when, sometime later, Seyss-Inquart, Hitler's overlord in the Netherlands, lashed out almost spitefully against the students, calling them, "good-for-nothing sons of plutocrats."

Then on February 6, 1943, the authorities carried out nationwide raids on the universities. Shortly thereafter came the announcement that those who wanted to continue their studies would have to sign a declaration of loyalty to the Nazi regime. Those who would not sign would be subject to forced labor in Germany. In the middle of April, when the signatures had to be in, only fifteen percent of the students had signed. By the end of April, those who hadn't signed were ordered to report for deportation to Germany. Rauter, the Gestapo High Commander, added that those who did not report would expose their parents to arrest and to further Gestapo measures.

I had been on the move since December, 1942. With the Gestapo harassing students, it seemed wise not to be too easily available. It was while staying with several relatives in Zeeland that I fell in love with Mies, a sweet, blue-eyed, blonde seventeen-year-old from Goes. It was love at first sight. I used every chance I could to get to know her, and, apparently, she felt the same. I met her at the train station as she came home from teachers' college each day and walked her home. Between the daisies and the blossoming orchards in the Zeeuwse polders, we discovered that our lives were meant to continue together, for better and for worse. It would be worse in the coming years. With the required declaration of loyalty, the situation took a very personal turn.

Our parents felt we were rushing matters, especially with the threat of Nazi arrest hanging over me. But that didn't matter to us.

I had done quite a bit of reading and thinking in the months in Zeeland, and my own convictions had grown: the battle against national socialism was not just a battle with arms; it was ideological, a religious battle, and I could not sign the declaration. Fortunately for my own peace of mind, in spite of Rauter's threat, my parents agreed. At eighteen years of age and financially dependent on them, their opinion carried quite some weight for me.

My parents had already been scouting around for a place for me to hide, a place not obviously connected to me or to my family. The rumors were getting stronger that Gestapo raids were at hand. Finally, one afternoon my mother came home, radiant. She had found such a place: the old watchmaker's shop owned by the ten Booms in downtown Haarlem where Corrie lived with her father and her older sister, Betsie. My mother knew Corrie quite well through their joint work in a church ministry for mentally handicapped children. When Corrie heard of my problem, she spontaneously offered hospitality and shelter for the time being: "He can stay with us until we find a more suitable place for him."

"We shall, of course, take care of your ration cards

for food," my mother told me. "We'll regularly pick up your dirty laundry and of course pay your board and lodging. It is an excellent place to hide, with two such nice innocent ladies and their old father. Fancy, he is over eighty and still does his watchmaker's work. You could not hope for a better place. Corrie said you can come tomorrow. I'll take care of your packing tonight."

I agreed, halfheartedly. My mother might be right about the innocence of this hiding place, but it did not strike me as very exciting, not with a war on our doorstep. But beggars can't be choosers. After all, in May, 1943, I was an outlaw.

In Hiding

2

I moved to the BéJé*, as the ten Booms called their busy house and shop, after sundown on May 13. Most of the time the German patrols stuck to the main roads, so in those twilight hours before curfew, I chose the narrow back streets to get to the watchmaker's shop on the Barteljorisstraat. That day my parents had taken most of the things I'd need so I could move quickly.

The only dangerous location, the corner of the Grote Markt near the town hall, was virtually deserted. When I turned left into the Barteljorisstraat, I

---

*The word (pronounced BAY-YAY) is an abbreviation of "Barteljorisstraat," the street on which the house is located.

saw only an elderly couple walking in the same direction further up the street. I could also see, on the right, the name, "ten Boom," on a window of the shop.

Carefully following instructions, I turned right into a narrow alley. It was empty so I pressed the button on the post of the green door. Quick steps sounded and the door opened. "Welcome! Come in, quickly," Corrie's cheerful voice greeted me.

"I am Tante Kees,*" she said, "and I do hope that you'll be very happy here." She led the way, turning left up a short staircase onto another landing where she opened a door into a small room. The curtains were drawn to prevent light from being seen from outside. In the middle was an oval table where a stately lady was busy with her sewing. To the right, next to the stove, sat an older man who could have passed for a patriarch. He had snow-white hair with a beautiful full white beard, and he looked at me over his gold-rimmed glasses.

"Father," Tante Kees said, "This is Hans. He will stay with us for some time." I didn't know who to address first—the lady or the obvious master of the house—but he solved the problem. "Well, my boy, we are glad that you trust us to offer you shelter, but we have to expect our ultimate protection from our Father in heaven. We do hope that our Lord will bless your stay. Sit down here."

He pointed to a chair next to him and I obediently sat down, but not before introducing myself to the lady at the table. She smiled and said, "I will be your Tante Bep* from now on. We cannot offer you much in the way of companionship of your own age, but we

---

*Tante Kees and Tante Bep were the names the family and others called Corrie and Betsie ten Boom respectively.

16

shall certainly get on well." Then, the patriarch started his interrogation. I had to tell him everything about myself—my background, my convictions, why I needed to hide. He was surprisingly sharp for his age, and he often interjected approving remarks. He left no doubt about his own views. Several of his grandsons faced the same threat.

When I told him about our refusal to sign the students' declaration of loyalty, he smiled mischievously. He turned out to be the chairman of the board of the Dreefschool (elementary and high school). Early in 1942 they had received orders from the national-socialist mayor of Haarlem to sign a declaration that the school didn't have any Jewish students. The old man had helped to achieve a unanimous board decision not to answer these summons. At his age he was still involved as much as I was.

Then, unexpectedly, at about 9:15, he said, "Children, it's time for an old man to go to bed. We shall say our evening prayers. Please, Bep, hand me the Bible." Only a slight raising of her eyebrows indicated that the request was something out of the ordinary, but she rose and, without comment, gave the old Bible to her father.

He leafed somewhere in the middle of the Bible and then started reading aloud. Immediately I recognized the age-old words of Psalm 121, what we called, "The Pilgrims' Psalm." We always read it in my home before starting out on a journey. "Where does my help come from? My help comes from the Lord, the Maker of heaven and earth." I looked across the table. The yellow circle of lamplight shone on my newly acquired aunts. Their hands were folded and they had a quiet, faraway look in their eyes

17

as Opa* read. "He will watch over your life; the Lord will watch over your coming and going both now and forevermore."

The old man folded his hands on his Bible and began to pray. Joint evening prayers were new to me. We said our evening prayers in private at my house. But here was someone with a personal line to heaven, talking in simple words to his Father, naming one by one all our concerns, trusting them to the Lord's care. "We pray for Piet de Koning and Goof Somson, from whom we have not heard for such a long time. Be near them wherever they may be. And we pray for Fred and Bob and Kik. Protect them; they need Your presence so much."

Names that I did not yet know, but that witnessed the involvement of this family, lacking so much in physical power but immensely strong in intercessory prayer for divine help. "We ask Your special blessing for our beloved Queen Wilhelmina on whose shoulders You have laid such a heavy burden. Be her strength so she can guide us according to Your will. But above all we pray that Your Son may return soon, in all His glory, and that we may be with Him forever, world without end. Amen!" With that he closed the Bible and rose.

Little did we know that with that simple gesture a chapter in our lives was closing and a new one was beginning. As he left the room he said, "Sleep well, my boy. Sleep well, children."

Tante Kees took me up three short winding stairs and down a corridor to the front of the house. "It's a complicated building," she explained, "because originally there were two houses. I'll show you around

---

*Opa is the Dutch pet name for grandfather

tomorrow, when it is light."

Passing a few sliding doors to rooms that could not be larger than cubicles, we came to a door at the end of the corridor. It opened into a furnished room which spanned the whole width of the house under the steeply inclined roof. It contained two beds and some closets formed by separating off some space under the roof at the sides of the room. "Stay away from the windows," she cautioned. "We have lace curtains, but the neighbors shouldn't notice anything out of the ordinary. Also, the shop and the workshop behind it are out of bounds for you. Customers in the shop must not see you. But make yourself at home as much as you like in this room," she urged and added, "Oh, Hans, I hope you will be happy here." By then I felt quite at home already, and I told her so. Tante Kees then indicated the other bed which had three mattresses on top of each other.

"We may get more guests like you, so you probably won't be alone in this room for long. Now please watch this." She lifted a slip of the curtain to show the black-out screen which hung between the curtain and the window. "Be careful never to switch on the light before you take the proper black-out precautions." She then led me back along the corridor and opened a door to a small cubicle with a cold water tap and a metal, white enamel wash basin. "You can wash here. It's somewhat primitive, but it will have to do for the time being."

I had camped out on several holidays and I reassured her. "Tante Kees, stop worrying! Everything I need is here. I'm just very grateful that you're willing to put up with me and take the risks that you do." A confident smile showed on her face.

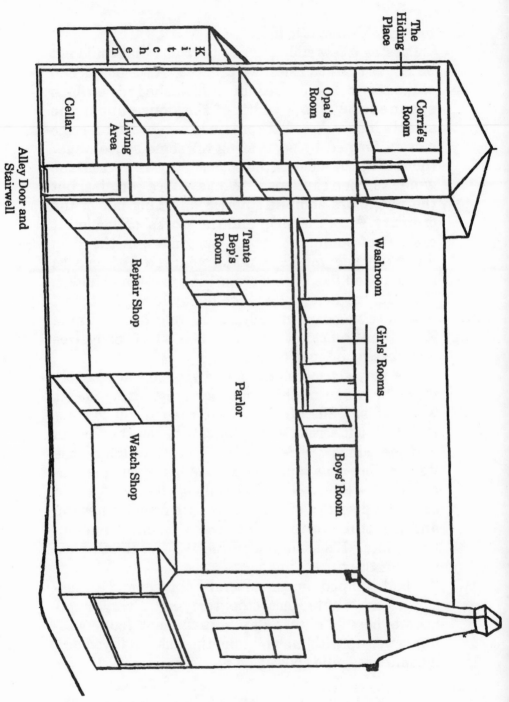

The Hiding Place

Corrie's Room

Opa's Room

Cellar

Living Area

Kitchen

Alley Door and Stairwell

Repair Shop

Tante Bep's Room

Washroom

Girls' Rooms

Watch Shop

Parlor

Boys' Room

20

"Now don't you worry either. The Lord has arranged His angels around this house and you'll be safe here." I must have appeared startled because she patted me on the back and said, "You don't believe that yet, do you? Just trust and you'll see the angels, just like Elisha's servant saw them standing protectively around them when the Lord opened his eyes."

Later as I lay in bed, seemingly right over my head, the Damiate bells of the old St. Bavo church started chiming. Their tune was well-known to every Haarlem citizen, and its familiarity was somehow comforting. The bells made it easier for me to accept such a drastic change in my life. My prayers were short that evening, but they included for the first time my new hosts who were willing to take such risks for me. My last thoughts were for my sweetheart: *I must write to her soon and tell her all about my new home.* But soon I was sound asleep. My free life had come to an end.

LIFE WITH THE
TEN BOOMS
3

In the next few weeks I quickly fell into an uneventful routine. I ate breakfast with Tante Kees about 7:30, and the first morning she explained why she was usually the first one up. She went to where the radio was hidden and tuned it to the BBC, trying to avoid the German jamming.

"Now, look at this," she said, as she brought out a large old-fashioned chain-watch. "At the first boom of Big Ben, it will be 8:00 a.m. to the second. At that moment I time the difference with this mother watch." While the Big Ben bells chimed their well-known tune, she followed the second hand closely. When the first boom sounded, the old watch was three seconds short of the hour. "Not bad!" Tante

23

Kees said. "Yesterday it was one second fast. It's an old watch, but it's never more than a few seconds off either way, summer or winter." Her pride showed clearly in her obvious satisfaction with this gem of her craft. "During the day this will be the standard for all other clocks and watches in the shop and in repair. It's the first thing I do every morning."

The ritual over, she then went to her bench in the work room behind the shop to start her daily routine of watch repair. Now fifty-one years old, she had learned the repair trade at a Swiss watchmakers' school some twenty-five years ago. The better I came to know her, the more I was amazed at the varying colors her lively personality revealed. Extreme precision and meticulous craftsmanship contrasted strongly with an easygoing, almost careless, approach to life.

Opa, as I learned to call the old man, and Tante Bep came down around 8:30, and soon the normal activities of the day began. After a light breakfast, Opa took his place next to the stove. But just as often he joined Tante Kees in the workshop. The most difficult repairs were still a challenge to him. I often saw him at his bench when I passed through the corridor behind the workshop. With the watchmakers' magnifying ocular in his left eye, his experienced hands moved quietly, without trembling, and with utmost care. But at eighty-four, he tired easily, and then he would retire to his favorite corner in the living room where he would sit reading for hours.

When we had lunch or dinner together, Opa quietly presided but left most of the talk to others. After meals he took his old Bible and his hymnal, *Liederen Uit de Schat van de Kerk der Eeuwen* (Hymns from the Heritage of the Christian Church) and he read to us the old-fashioned words. We could hear the faith of the Bible authors and poets resonating in his voice. Their agonies and their joys, their trust and their faith were his. Their God was his God and, with an unshakable faith, he entrusted his life and soul into his Father's hands, silently challenging us to do the same. Likewise, in the usual evening prayers, it was again amazing how this frail old man, in his corner next to the stove, unfailingly picked up the deeper concerns and emotions of the busy people around him. Often he prayed for friends who had been arrested or deported or who were in concentration camps—whose fate simply was not known.

Not only had Opa been brought up in a deeply religious family, but he had been made intensely aware of the special place the Jews have in God's plan for the world.

Long before his birth, his father, Willem, had been part of a religious revival which had as one of its main spokesmen, a Christian Sephardic Jew named Isaac da Costa. And not only did the family take a fervent biblical stand against the current modernistic theology that had become mainstream in the Reformed Church, but they witnessed of the Old Testament promises of God for the dispersed Jews. For Grandfather, love for Jews was second nature, and he passed this on to his four children and his grandchildren.

One day while walking through the Barteljorisstraat with grandson, Peter, they passed the well-known watch shop of Mr. Kan. Noticing the watches, Peter inquired of his grandfather, "Is Mr. Kan a competitor of yours?" Grandfather stopped, looked down at Peter, and said quietly, "Son, Mr. Kan is a colleague of mine, and, moreover, he is a son of God's chosen people. Don't you ever forget that."

Just after I arrived, Tante Kees told me how Opa had gone to the town hall along with the Jewish citizens of Haarlem to get one of the yellow Stars of David the Jews were required to sew on their coat. When he asked Tante Bep to sew it on his coat, his daughters protested. "If God's people must suffer, then I will suffer," he insisted. Only with great difficulty had they persuaded him that the gesture, however laudable, would not help his Jewish friends, and might only create unnecessary problems.

For all of us under Opa's roof, his prayers became a continuing powerful source of trust and hope. Without this, we might not have survived emotionally and spiritually. Later, when I was arrested, I realized that this trust reached far beyond Tante Kees' faith in protecting angels; it was an unconditional commitment of oneself into God's hands. Their love for God's chosen people made the ten Booms respect any of the convictions of the Jews they sheltered; they never abused the integrity of their guests by attempting to convert them. They had many animated discussions, to be sure, but they considered their daily life to be a sufficient example of their faith in Christ.

Tante Bep arranged the domestic work in this not-so-average Dutch household, and I became an expert at peeling potatoes and washing the dishes. "Perhaps you can also teach me the fine art of cooking," I suggested to her one day. "I can try to get some new potatoes from Zeeland through my relatives there."

"That would be great!" Tante Bep replied. "With these old potatoes we can't prepare anything better than a plain Dutch meal and certainly no haute cuisine."

For all her courageous spirit, her pallor witnessed the severe anemia she had suffered all her life. At fifty-eight she couldn't stand much strain. She wore rather sober dresses and a small velvet neck-band, and during the day, a large white domestic apron protected them from the risks of the gas range or the sink. Day-to-day work she took on, moving quietly at her own pace. During the afternoon she rested, often for quite some time. It was natural, therefore, that I took on the heavier chores such as housecleaning and shoveling coal. And there was much of it. The BéJé, like so many centuries-old Dutch houses, had no modern conveniences such as central heating or bath or shower. There was a coal stove in the living room and in the parlor, a toilet in the basement and on the second floor, and a cold water tap in the boys' room. For all the others there was the usual wash bowl and water jug.

When more "guests" arrived, Tante Bep was quickly relieved of all matters but those of herself or family. It remained for her to indicate her schedule for the day and to take care that things were done properly (meaning *her* way). And she came to relish the relief. It gave her more time to enjoy the pleasant companionship of her family.

During shop hours, two others were part of the regular ten Boom household. Mr. Ineke, as we called him, was the experienced assistant for watch and clock repairs. He had served with the ten Booms for quite some time, but he always kept in the background. One could always find him in the repair shop behind his workbench, his head bowed while the lamp shone on his hands, deftly working on the tiny parts of the complicated mechanisms.

Henny van Dantzig was the saleswoman in the shop. Well into her thirties, pleasant and outgoing, she had a cheerful word for everyone. She had been with the family through all the years of the economic depression, and she had shared with them many of their problems of living on limited means. In a sense she had become part of the family.

Opa in particular had a special place in her heart. When he was around, she was the first to jump up to answer a small request that he might have. She arranged his tools, often guessing his needs. He, in turn, enjoyed her warm-hearted presence. She told me how he had come to her one morning in utter despair. While working at his bench, a tiny screw had sprung from between his tweezers and lodged itself in his beard, and he had been unable to retrieve it. After she finished laughing, she was able to find the missing piece.

All those who found shelter with the ten Booms soon felt at home with Henny. Her trustworthiness and alertness gave us an effective early warning system if she spotted possible danger outside.

Then there was the family cat, pitch-black Snoetje. Not afraid of the many people who were often around, she roamed the entire house at her pleasure. But she spent most of the time in the living room or the kitchen where she could find company and food. When our numbers grew and eight or ten of us sat around the table for lunch, Snoetje would step from shoulder to shoulder, graciously accepting handouts at each stop. Opa unerringly found a biblical nickname for her: Maher-Shalal-Hash-Baz: "fast to grab the spoils" (Isaiah 8:3).

Hansje Frankfort-Israels, or Thea, as she was

called, arrived the day after I did. She had been hiding in another place that had become too dangerous. She was withdrawn, almost silent at first, but Opa's sincere interest finally won her over. It was he who got her to tell her story.

She and her husband had lived and worked at a clinic called Het Apeldoornsche Bosch, where they nursed mentally retarded Jews. They were happy with their lives, and although the patients didn't understand much they trusted the staff. Then, unexpectedly, the previous January the Germans raided the place and began to kick the patients and beat them. At first the patients thought it was a party, but when the blood began to flow, they became scared. "I have never seen such haunted looks," Thea told us. "The Germans took those poor people outside and herded them through the gate with shouts and sticks toward railroad cars designed for cattle transport. Then they stacked them one on top of the other and carried them off to Germany. Many of them were dead before they crossed the border."

We were shocked. Tante Bep had tears in her eyes. Tante Kees' fists were clenched by the time Thea finished her tale. Unable to help their patients, she and her husband fled. They managed to escape arrest, but they had been on the run since that awful day. To find shelter, they had to separate. For some time now she had not heard anything about him.

The quiet and trusting atmosphere at the BéJé worked miracles and Thea quickly became her cheerful self again. As a non-observant Jew, she had no problems in temporarily adjusting to a Christian home. Helping others turned out to be not only her profession but also her nature, and I soon discovered

29

the fun of sharing the daily work load with her.

At first I used my spare time to study a few subjects such as math. Under the circumstances, however, differential calculus seemed pointless, so I gave up
before long and passed the time chatting or dis-
cussing issues with the others, playing chess, listening to music, reading, and writing. I had tacked a picture of my fiancée to the wall next to my bed, and I
spent long hours there writing to her the continuing
story of my life underground. I couldn't tell her open-
ly where I was, but I could describe the events vividly
enough while writing an innocent letter. It also provided a safety valve for my bottled-up emotions.
Each night her picture was the last sight I saw before
switching off the light.

One Sunday in May many of the ten Boom family
gathered during the afternoon to celebrate Opa's
eighty-fourth birthday. Nollie van Woerden, the third
ten Boom sister, lived in Haarlem some fifteen minutes away by bike, and she came with her husband,
Flip, and her family. So did Willem, the only ten
Boom son and a minister of the Reformed church in
Hilversum.

When I tried to slip away upstairs, Tante Kees
caught me. "Hans, why don't you come in and meet
our family?" After I had been properly introduced,
she unexpectedly said to her brother, "Hans is staying with us, but I think he will be bored here before
long. Do you know someone in the country who can
use an extra pair of hands on the farm? You have
good connections. I can tell you now that he is easy
to get along with."

Willem, taken aback, didn't answer immediately, so she went on cheerfully. "Oh, not to worry. You just think about it. Ask your son, Kik, to help you." Between the two of you, you should be able to come up with something." I must have looked surprised because Willem scolded her. "One of your spur of the moment schemes again, Corrie? Shouldn't we ask Hans himself if he would appreciate that? Why should he not want to stay here? He seems well settled."

She said, however, quite seriously, "There is more to it. You know, I've been thinking about what Thea told us. There will be much need for shelter for our Jewish people. There will always be more Dutchmen who will provide a home to non-Jews than to Jews. We are willing to help Jews, so let us shelter as many as we can. Wouldn't you agree?" When Willem nodded thoughtfully, Tante Kees pressed her advantage. "You will try for him, won't you?"

So Willem asked me some necessary details, and I finally left, with his promise that he would shop around. "But do not expect anything overnight," he cautioned. That was fine with me; I was happy with life as it was.

"Seek Ye First..."
4

On the same day I went into hiding, the Germans ordered Dutch citizens to turn in all radios. The ten Booms still had an old antiquated model with a separate loudspeaker that they had stashed away in a closet. It carried a lot of sentimental value, and Tante Bep in particular hated to part with it. But by turning that in, they could secretly keep their second radio, a smaller model which could easily be hidden.

On the afternoon that Tante Kees took the old one to the collection center, she came home very upset. "The sergeant on duty asked me if we had any more radios at home," she told us, "and I said 'No,' loud and clear, just like that. I lied! Now I can't understand how I did that so easily." Lying was so completely against her upbringing that she was shocked at herself. Opa didn't respond at the moment, but for the Bible reading after dinner, he read the story of Rahab who saved the Israelite spies by hiding them and by lying to the search party. I guessed that this set Tante Kees' mind at rest, because she listened to the other radio happily after that.

Most of the time the job of listening to the news fell to me. Quickly I developed a sort of private shorthand for writing down the events so I could give a fairly complete report to those waiting downstairs. Then we discussed each bit of news, such as the progress of the war, statements from our government or from our own occupied country, and we compared these with previous information. We all tried to read between the lines. Eagerly we searched for the good news: the invasion of Western Europe that would end the murderous German rule.

At the end of the news one evening I picked up a one-word message: navigare, which means, "sailing." It was obviously a code for someone or something and it led to intense speculation downstairs. Did it indicate a move across the water? If it did have any consequences, we didn't hear about them. The voices of BBC news readers, such as Alan Howland, Frank Phillips, or Bruce Belfridge, became as familiar as those of trusted friends. And we received daily encouragement from the parting thought of Radio *Oranje*, the Dutch voice of freedom, on the BBC broadcast:

> *Though dark be the day and sad our separation,*
> *We've come one day closer to our liberation.*

News was more important than almost anything

34

else, so meals and domestic activities were scheduled around broadcasts. On the morning of Ascension Day we had gathered in the parlor, duties over, enjoying a recording of Schweitzer's rendition of *Nun danket Allen Gott* (Now Thank We All Our God), when suddenly, Opa, of all persons, interrupted. "It's radio time, my boy." When I reported back fifteen minutes later, he smiled mischievously. "You would have forgotten it!" We could trust him, even at eighty-four, not to forget the news.

Once or twice a week my mother visited Corrie to prepare for their next club meeting. Then she usually brought me clean laundry, various bits of news, and anything I needed. I looked forward to her visits so much because she was my personal go-between with the life I had left behind. Above all, she was the contact with my sweetheart. Every now and then she would bring the special letter I had waited for for days on end. Those letters brought new hope and new determination without which I could hardly survive.

Then one morning in May she brought a surprise. Out of its holder I unrolled a copy of the Dutch national anthem, the *Wilhelmus*. It was illegally printed and sold, the proceeds going to help those hiding from the Nazis. It must have cost her quite a bit. "Look at this, Tante Kees," I raved, spreading out the roll on the table in the living room.

"I think, my boy, it is fitting to read it aloud to all of us," Opa said. Embarrassed at the beginning, my voice gained confidence with the stately cadence of the fifteen stanzas. The hymn dates back more than four hundred years to William of Orange's fight for

35

religious freedom for the Low Countries under Spanish rule. Now its old words took on a new and very personal meaning for each of us. William believed fervently that his cause was just. He had a deep trust that the Almighty would vindicate the struggle and the sacrifices, and the words echoed our own situation.

> *But unto God, the greatest*
> *of Majesties, I owe*
> *obedience, first and latest,*
> *For justice wills it so.*

Opa saw my emotional involvement and he smiled. "Do you realize, my boy, that this also is true for our loyalty to our queen?" he gently asked. I looked at him, not understanding what he meant. "God forbid, but if she would demand from us an obedience beyond what God's Word tells us, our allegiance should be with our Father in heaven. We should then obey Him rather than her. However," he added quickly, seeing the shocked expression on my face, "don't be anxious. I expect her to serve the coming of His Kingdom rather than her own goals."

I was shocked indeed, but I realized at the same time that Opa was right again. He was warning me not to identify my loyalty to Queen Wilhelmina, at present the symbol for everything we yearned for, with my ultimate loyalty to our God and our Savior. Opa lifted my view from all too human values towards God and his Kingdom. I nodded, grateful for this perspective.

Later I tacked the document to the sloping roof under which I slept, and before long I knew it by heart, all fifteen stanzas. It became another source of power, recharging my batteries when confidence was low.

Toward the end of May my mother brought our old typewriter to the ten Boom's house. This finally gave me some new possibilities which I had been looking for. While I couldn't join in any outside subversive activity, I could at least assist in the underground pamphlet network. More and more underground newsletters and bulletins served as duty calls to those who too long had complied with—even accommodated—Nazi oppression. Each carbon copy meant one more appeal to resist the enemy. "Multiply and pass on!" was the password.

Soon I was busy during the afternoons. Many trusted visitors to the BéJé carried my typed copies of illegal prose, poems, protests, squibs, pedestrian rhymes, and poignant texts to the outside. And often they brought in new samples to be copied.

One afternoon while I was banging away at my typewriter, Tante Kees came up to my room. "Hans, I just had a customer who works at the town hall. He brought a watch for repair, but he also told how troubled he had become. The Germans are requiring more and more cooperation from the town hall staff. It seems that now they will have to give the Nazis the addresses of young men in those age groups that are required for forced labor in Germany. He feels that the moment might be at hand when he must draw the line. He showed me an illegal pamphlet, a farewell address from a Dutch government official who resigned because he couldn't accept the German treatment of the Jews. I thought you'd like to copy it, so he let me borrow it for a day."

She handed me a sheet of paper and I started reading. "Listen to this," I cried, getting more excited as it unfolded. "This is really great, Tante Kees."

37

I feel the need to explain briefly to you, as my staff, what has been the motive for handing in my resignation on September 12, 1940. That day it became clear to me that in our country the so-called 'Aryan declaration' will become mandatory. This means that, when considering applications or planning staff moves, we shall be obliged to investigate whether the person involved is of Jewish descent. However dear my vocation may be to me, because of this measure I felt obliged to hand in my resignation, as my conscience as a Christian and as a Dutchman will never allow me to put this question to anyone ever.

Any preference for one man over another because of his belonging to a certain race or people radically conflicts with the fundamentals of faith in Jesus Christ in Whom God, the Almighty Creator of Heaven and Earth, reveals Himself to mankind and before Whom all men are equal. But furthermore, the discrimination of the Jewish people in particular conflicts with God's Holy Word and His gospel because it has pleased God's infinite and unfathomable wisdom to offer salvation to all peoples and races through Jesus Christ, in the flesh a Son of this Jewish people. Any rejection of this people is inherently a rejection of Him.

As this is my deepest conviction, it will be clear that I, before God and my conscience, can never cooperate in any enforcement of the above measure . . . .

Finally, I would like to stress that through faith I realize that, beyond war and strife, the call of this gospel of Jesus Christ reaches out to every person individually, and to all peoples and races alike, and that there I do not distinguish friend or foe, be it Dutchman, German or Jew. We all need as our breath of life God's mercy and forgiveness in Jesus Christ.

I do not know my future, like none of you does, but nobody needs to be concerned because, while I know that I am powerless, I may expect all power from Him Who never forsakes us, even in the deepest distress.

When I finished I sat in silence. "I will multiply this carefully," I told Tante Kees. "When your customer returns, I'll have a number of copies ready for him to hand out to his colleagues at the town hall. And I'll add a few underground poems. That may help those who are undecided." With a smile, Tante Kees left the room. She had achieved her goal.

The days passed, seemingly quietly and orderly, but actually under mounting tension of worsening news of arrests and of disappointing news of the war. The invasion did not come and allied army progress was dishearteningly slow.

Air-raid warnings became routine and we soon stopped worrying about them, but the drone of the bomber engines never failed to excite us. There was "our side" on its way to bring the war home to the Germans themselves. And when the anti-aircraft fire became less intense over the weeks, we saw it as a sign that we were gaining supremacy in the air.

It also dawned on our household during that time that our plight might last longer than we originally thought. In our hopeful optimism, we still made bets that the invasion would come next week, but deep down we gradually realized that the suffering of the occupied countries probably carried very little weight in the great war plan of the Allied Forces.

"They cannot risk failure," a visitor to the BéJé said one day during a discussion in the parlor. "They might then sacrifice as many as a hundred thousand of their own men, and it would lay us open to much more dramatic German measures, like the deportation of our whole population to Poland, for instance. So they have to take their time, to build up such a massive force that an invasion will not fail." Though our minds agreed with this reasoning, our hearts certainly did not.

However, it did make us realize that we should seriously prepare for a lengthy siege, not only mentally but physically. Our hiding place could be betrayed; we had to take precautionary measures, quickly.

The Germans themselves made this very clear when, on June 8, they carried out mass arrests of young men all over the country. They arrested hundreds and transported them to Germany to work in the war industry.

The same raids brought Mary van Itallie, another Jewish lady to us. She was forty-two years old, slender and fragile, the daughter of a professor at the University of Amsterdam. Well-educated, she had been the director of an Italian travel agency in Amsterdam and had been exempted from transport to Germany until now. But time was running out for her, too, and friends persuaded her to seek shelter in time. At the beginning of the German persecution of the Dutch Jewish population, Mary's parents committed suicide to escape a worse fate. Although she knew more or less what might be ahead, she refused to accept defeat. She believed strongly in the ultimate victory of goodness, truth, and beauty, and her positive attitude helped us all very much.

The restrictions of freedom and privacy while in hiding must have contrasted starkly with her former, rather sophisticated existence. In her previous hiding place, she had had to share a bed for a few nights with the daughter of her hosts. "It was a physical and cultural shock," she confided, smiling but still horrified. However, she adjusted graciously and gratefully to the sober lifestyle of the ten Booms.

Two young, single Dutchmen—Henk Wessels and Leendert Kip—arrived shortly after Mary. Both of them, I assumed, were hiding to avoid conscription, but I had learned that it was safer not to ask too many questions. I knew only what those in hiding volunteered about themselves. Henk was a quiet but cheerful fellow, but Leendert was active, always ready to voice an opinion or begin a discussion.

As a group we realized we had to take urgent safety measures, so after repeated inspections of the house, we chose the attic as an emergency hideout. It wasn't ideal but at the time it seemed acceptable. I offered to clean the place but regretted it immediately.

"Thea, look at this," I called down from the pitch-dark space up high between the rafters.

Thea, who was vacuuming the top floor, put her head through the access hatch. "For crying out loud," she gasped, looking at the one-and-a-half-inch layer of dust that had accumulated on the attic floor over the ages. "Wait!" She scrambled off the ladder, ran downstairs and came back with a scarf and one of

Tante Bep's old aprons. "Put these on. It should help some." In no time I was dirty all over.

We sawed a hatch in a less obvious place and nailed the original one shut, but it was all in vain. When we started an emergency drill, we quickly realized the attic was no good at all. It would take too much precious time to get up there and close the hatch. It just didn't work and we admitted that we needed expert advice.

Tante Kees solved the problem. "I'll ask Pickwick," she said. "I'm sure he'll know someone who can help us." Herman Slurink, was an old and rich friend whose physical likeness to Dickens' Pickwick character had earned him the nickname. Within two days he sent an architect who rejected the attic immediately. So what then? Where were we to create a hiding place for six to nine adults?

Finally, the architect decided on a false wall in Tante Kees' bedroom. "This is the place," he said. "We shall make a false wall here." He measured about two feet from the outside wall into her room. "One layer of bricks will be enough. A fake closet at the left in front of it and a sliding panel in the back of the closet should do it. My lady, this will be great. I'll be just as proud of this as of the beautiful houses I've built. Do you mind sacrificing part of your room?"

Tante Kees readily agreed. "There will be enough room left for my bed, and I can help people get behind the wall if there is an emergency."

We lost no time making the arrangements. Leendert, always full of ideas, wired a set of alarm buzzers that could be triggered by push-buttons in the shop, near the side door to the alley. We could hear them all over the house. The next Monday a trusted contractor brought the first batch of bricks and cement. Several neighbors noticed them, but Tante Bep satisfied their curiosity. "We've lived here so long that we need some modern facilities," she told them. The neighbors left, convinced that the ten Booms were probably building a new bathroom and that Tante Bep was too prudish to say so.

In two days the false wall and closet were ready, and one brick was taken out of the outside wall to allow some fresh air. A sliding panel some three feet wide and two feet high formed the lower part of the back of the closet. It slid in tight-fitting grooves so that no cracks or slits would show when the panel was closed. A cord over a wheel and a counterweight made it move easily. Wall and closet were painted the next day and the smell of fresh paint was noticeable for several days.

On Saturday, Tante Kees put her things into the closet. Nothing indicated that a secret hiding place existed behind that normal, innocent wall. Only by looking left out of the window of Tante Kees' room could an observant person spot the extension of the house beyond the wall. Indeed, just as the architect predicted, the hiding place was a jewel. We were so proud of it, and within hours we christened it the Angels' Den. We had heard rumors that the Gestapo was planning mass arrests over the weekend, so that same day we began to practice. First, we decided to leave the panel open all day. After we were all inside, Tante Kees would place two large sewing boxes in the bottom compartment so the closet would look normal.

We greased the grooves of the panel and improved the balance. We stuck a rubber strip to the bottom to muffle the sound in case of a hurried closing. We had some doubts about the fresh air supply but we left that to decide later. Two mattresses served to dampen possible sounds. A metal container in the corner would serve for calls of nature. The house, when raided, should not show signs of anyone else except the ten Booms. Therefore, we reduced personal items such as extra clothing to a minimum. Ladies' dresses were stored innocently in the wardrooms of the aunts. Before retiring every night we stored our clothes and suitcases in the secret room so that in the event of an emergency, we would not have to carry much. In the morning we left pajamas and nightgowns there so they wouldn't betray us.

Saturday night, June 2, we had our first drill. Without warning Tante Kees rang the alarm. We jumped out of bed, folded our blankets, turned our mattresses, and scrambled through the corridor. Tante Kees stood ready, stopwatch in hand, guiding us through the opening. We lowered the panel and she put the sewing boxes in front of it, sat down on her bed, and stopped her watch. "Three minutes, twenty-eight seconds," she shouted, aghast. We heard it through the false wall, standing close to each other. We felt so let down. In spite of all the preparations, a Gestapo raid would never allow us three-and-a-half minutes. Some delay at the shop entrance and some preliminary searching of the lower floors might give us a minute and a half, but that would be the limit.

One by one we crawled out and sat on the floor in our pajamas, utterly dejected. "One minute and a half should be our deadline," Tante Kees decided and we agreed. A few seconds could mean the difference between survival or arrest.

"Let's run through all the actions and see where we can save time," Leendert suggested, so, wearily, we went through the motions again, one by one.

Turning the mattresses and entering the secret room took most of the time, so I suggested that I sleep in the Angels' Den. "That would mean one less person to evacuate," I argued. "I could also store the stuff you carry. Everybody could then crawl in much easier."

We all looked questioningly toward Tante Kees. She'd have to give up her privacy. But without hesitation she asked, "Hans, won't you be cold in there so close to the outer wall?"

"Well, we can put in some blankets," I replied. "We'll need them anyway when winter comes."

"All right, then; it's settled," she sighed. "We'll have to figure out a go-to-bed routine. Who knows, that may even be fun!" Her spirit rose to the occasion. "Now let's inspect the rooms before we have another exercise."

One by one we critically examined each room. "Hans, you'll have to take down that picture of your fiancée." I agreed, not very happy about it, but I realized that such an innocent picture could give us away. "Now, off to bed, and we'll have another drill later."

This time we were much more careful to clean up. I moved with my blankets and clothes into the Angels' Den. A small lamp dimly lit the corridor, and quiet once again reigned over the house.

Suddenly the alarm buzzer sounded and I woke up dazed. Within seconds I folded my blankets and stood ready near the entrance. Thea was the first to arrive; she threw her small night bag inside and started to crawl in. I picked up her bag and helped pull her

45

inside. "Keep moving to the end," I whispered to her. Mary followed. She was slender and slid in easily. I knew she was particular about her belongings, so I put her bag back in her hands while helping her up. "Move on until you feel Thea," I told her as quietly as I could, while helping Leendert and picking up his briefcase. When Henk had slipped in, I slid the panel down and stood up. A scraping sound indicated that Tante Kees had replaced her sewing boxes. We were quiet, not knowing if this was just a drill or a real alarm. "Come this way a bit," I whispered to Henk. "If they shoot through the panel, then at least they won't hurt you."

"Hans, stop it. Don't say those things," Mary said in a muffled voice. "I know you're right, but I hate it, I hate it." I felt her shivering against my shoulder.

"Girls, you sit down for a bit," Leendert suggested. "That way you'll stick it out much longer. We can take turns." Mary and Thea slid to the floor. There were no sounds from the outside. We heard a car stop somewhere, then drive on again.

Henk whispered, "We don't have any food here—another thing we overlooked! Let's make a list tomorrow."

Suddenly we heard quick steps approaching Tante Kees' room. We held our breath. Then Tante Kees' cheerful voice broke the tension. "All right, you can come out now. Two minutes, four seconds this time." But we couldn't immediately adjust to her enthusiasm. We had improved our performance but we were badly shaken. It was no longer a game; it was now serious business. "I've inspected the rooms," she went on, "and Tante Bep is making hot chocolate. Come along!"

46

Quietly we filed out of the room and down to the living room and over the hot chocolate discussed the exercise. Tante Kees and Leendert did most of the talking. Thea and Mary just sat there, pale, listening, readily agreeing to the suggestions. I didn't have much to say, either. For the first time I had experienced real fear.

In the course of the days the drills became routine, lacking the tension of the first ones. Tante Bep promised cream puffs every time we could make it within ninety seconds. In the end, hiding during the daytime took us about sixty seconds, but at night we needed seventy seconds. The cream puffs, so easily promised, proved to be difficult to get. They were also quite expensive, so the treat was soon forgotten.

We had made the mark and had become real experts at hiding, and the hiding place had become an essential part of our lives. We put the radio in there as well, simplifying the situation, and the boys took turns sleeping in the "Angels' Den." We gave a crash training course to every newcomer, so that a change in crew would not endanger our ship. Gradually we became confident that we could beat the Gestapo at its own game of hide and seek.

Eusi came to us on Monday, June 28, my birthday. The day had begun at 7:00 when Tante Kees came into the boys' room with a "Rise and shine, rise and shine." At breakfast they presented me with a book and everybody sang the traditional Dutch birthday song, *Lang zal hij leven* (Long Shall He Live).

Roused by the commotion that took place right under his bedroom, Opa came down early and wished me, "God speed, my boy. Always be true to your convictions. Serve the Lord and don't forget, be loyal to our queen!"

But the best present came towards the end of the afternoon when my parents brought a letter from Mies, my sweetheart. It was too risky, all had agreed, for us to write more than once a month, but we could write as many pages as we wished in each letter. The strengthening words in those pages brought new confidence and hope for me and made my day.

Two van Woerden daughters, Aty and Cockie, joined us directly after dinner and we had an evening full of chatter and laughter. In spite of the circumstances, it was almost a carefree affair.

Around 8:00 the doorbell rang. Tante Kees had told us that she was expecting a new guest, so the interruption didn't create anxiety. When she came back a few minutes later with a man in his mid-30's, there was no doubt in our minds. His Jewish background was written all over him.

Before she could introduce him, however, the newcomer pointed to Opa and exclaimed, "Is that your father? Why, if he were Jewish, he might be a patriarch."

Opa, obviously pleased by such recognition, answered kindly, "Sir, we may be God's children by grace, but you are a son of His chosen people by birthright." And with that a mutual appreciation was born.

Soon the new guest was the center of conversation. He was Meijer Mossel, the cantor of the Jewish Community in Amsterdam. "Yes, yes, I was *chazzan*, (cantor) for sure," he told us. "But now? Am I a *chazzan?* Where is my Torah? Where is my *shul* (synagogue)? Where is my congregation? The *goyim*, the

Gentiles, have laid the city to waste. They have come for the children of Zion. They have come to destroy us. You ask why I did not go to the Joodse Schouwburg* when the summons came? Why my wife and family did not go? I'll tell you why. My only purpose in life is to sing praises to Adonai, the Lord. I am a *Yehude,* a *Yid.* That means one who praises Adonai. Can I praise Adonai when they have killed me? Then I would be a martyr, yes, but can a martyr sing the praise of Adonai? So, *hinneh,* here I am, at your mercy." Then he turned to Opa and asked, "You will allow me to say my prayers and sing my praises in this house?"

We listened, amazed. Here was someone who knew why he did what he did, not out of fear of dying, but for a higher purpose. Tante Kees answered him. "Of course you can say your prayers here. Why don't you use the boys' room? There you can be on your own, at your own convenience. You will sleep there with Leendert, Henk, and Hans. They don't use the room during the day." Meijer Mossel nodded gratefully, and Tante Kees continued. "But if you insist on living kosher we are in big trouble. According to your standards, everything in this house is unclean."

"Madam," he responded, "Don't you worry. As the Almighty—blessed be His name—is my witness, I would like nothing better than to eat kosher and to live kosher and to live in peace with my own people. But these are bad times, times of oppression. Adonai allows the Huns to persecute my people. In such times He feeds us in His way. Remember Elijah? You must

---

*The location where Jewish citizens had to assemble when they received a summons to report for transportation to the east.

know this story from your Bible.

"He was on the run, and the Master of the Universe fed him, first through ravens and later through a widow from the Gentiles. Was that food kosher? Should I rather starve and die, or eat non-kosher and live to praise my Master? Your food will be my pleasure, Madam!"

Obviously relieved, Tante Kees switched to another topic. "Fine, then that will be no problem. But please stop calling me 'Madam.' Everybody here calls me Tante Kees. Would you mind doing the same? And now," she continued, "we have to find a name for you. Do you have any preference?"

The cantor laughed. "My people call me "Meijer." With that name I was born and with that name I shall die. Should I then care what name you would remember me by? Why not Winston or Wolfgang? It won't change my loyalties." After several suggestions, Meijer turned to me and said, "It is your birthday, I understand. Would you do me the favor of naming me?"

The request was a complete surprise, but I had an answer: "Well, Sir, we'll call you Eusi."

"Eusi, Eusi," he mused, saying it as if tasting the name. "Where do you get that?" he asked.

"Oh, it's just a kind of pet name for the youngest member of the family," I replied. "In my home—and in my friend's home—everyone calls the youngest brother Eusi. It doesn't mean anything in particular."

"But what if you add more members to this household?" He smiled, slyly. "Then will I no longer be junior?"

"No," I answered, "you will stay Eusi for us. Once a name, always a name. Besides, for the next one maybe someone else will have a birthday and have the honor of naming that person."

"All right, Eusi it will be," he said. Then, with a graceful bow he turned to Tante Bep. "My lady, allow me to introduce myself. I am Eusi. And you have earned my lasting gratitude by accepting me into your home."

Probably too tired to share in the general laughter, she smiled back and replied wanly, "Welcome here, Eusi. May your stay be a happy one for all of us. And please, call me Tante Bep, like the others do."

Later in the evening, after another of our regular drills, Opa called us for the evening prayers. "What's that?" Eusi inquired. I explained and Eusi said, "Please, Hans, apologize for me for not attending. I shall say my own prayers here in the meantime. Tell them I will pray for protection for this home." The group, especially Opa, was visibly disappointed. But a few days later, Eusi joined us for evening prayers.

The crisis came on Eusi's second day with us. We had been quite busy with domestic routines and the breaking in of Eusi, interrupted by several emergency drills. It was a special day, the birthday of Prince Bernhard, husband of our Crown Princess Juliana. Tante Bep produced orange lemonade and we all cheered, wishing the prince many happy returns and a speedy return with his family to the Netherlands.

In the evening as we gathered in the parlor, we listened to a radio broadcast of the christening of our youngest Princess Margriet, in Ottawa, Canada. We listened silently, each steeped in his or her own thoughts, and when the broadcast was over, Opa said, "Children, this occasion calls for God's blessing. Let's all join in *Dat's Heeren zegen op u daal*" (Our

Good Lord Bless Thee from Above). Eusi was suspicious of anything a Christian might spring on him, but when he heard Opa read the Old Testament blessing from Psalm 134, he recognized the words and followed them closely, softly chanting the Hebrew text, moving his body rhythmically back and forth.

"What Opa read was certainly not the original text," he said, smiling, "but it will do." Then he grabbed a hymn book and enthusiastically joined in the singing.

It was a chance remark by Leendert that began a vehement discussion. Several days before that, Nollie van Woerden had said that if she were asked whether she was sheltering Jews, she would answer, "Yes!" She considered the Lord's decree, "You shall not lie," an absolute command which she would have to obey. She said she trusted that the Lord Who had guided her to offer shelter to the hunted would also take care of any situation that would result from her obedience to His command. Tante Kees had started preparing hot chocolate for us when Leendert commented on Nollie's remarks, and Eusi, who did not yet know the ten Booms that well, could not believe his ears.

"Tell me I did not hear you correctly. Tell me I misunderstood. Do I hear that she would betray her Jids to the Gestapo? Do I hear that she would rather sacrifice lives than lie?" His voice rose in anger and he stood up as he spoke. He looked as if he would explode in outrage.

Tante Kees heard the commotion from the kitchen and came rushing into the living room. "Sh, be quiet, be quiet," she pleaded. "Eusi, please sit down, and let's talk about this."

He sat down but spat out, "What is there to talk

about? Lives are at stake, and you want to talk."

We all watched Tante Kees, uncertain of what would follow. I knew the ten Boom's attitude towards the Nazis and towards "God's chosen people," as Opa lovingly called them. But Eusi didn't, yet. "You know God's commandment, 'You shall not give false testimony,' as well as we do," Tante Kees started, in a halfhearted attempt to argue her sister's position. But Eusi did not let her finish.

"Yes, yes, I expected that. But the Almighty—blessed be His name—gave those decrees to my people, telling them how to live as a nation in a land where His righteousness would reign. He wants us to worship Him and to live justly with our neighbors. But do we live under a just rule? We are ruled by terror and by fear. Woman, do you know fear, real fear for your very life? Have you seen the fear for the Huns in the eyes of the hunted? Have you been in the houses of those in Amsterdam who killed themselves? They did that because they didn't want to live again through the same horrors of five years ago in Germany. Woman, don't you realize lives are at stake? I would lie and steal and, yes, I would kill, to save those lives."

He was almost out of breath, yet he did not give Tante Kees a chance to say anything. "You want to live by the book, by what you call the Bible. But don't you see that in this way you just live by words from that book? The way your sister uses these words they may even kill. That is not what the Almighty—blessed be His name—wants. That is not serving God. Read your book, woman! You'll find stories, many stories, in which the Almighty blesses lies. But those lies helped His cause. Read what Samuel says, or Moses, before the King of Egypt, or Rahab." Suddenly he smiled. "Ha, I can do even better than that. Get your Bible. Right at the beginning of the second book of the Torah, what do you call that?

"Exodus," Tante Kees answered somewhat lamely, uncertain at his sudden change of mood. He started muttering the Hebrew text he knew by heart.

"You'll read there about two Hebrew midwives, Shiphrah and Puah, blessed be their memory. They deceived the King of Egypt; they lied to him and thus saved Hebrew babies. And what do you read? The Almighty blessed these midwives. See what I mean?" His indignation spent, he smiled again, sensing that they were on common ground.

"But," he continued, "here we are, under your roof. We have trusted our lives to you, Tante Kees. I demand that you tell us that you will not betray us, if you can help it. If I can't trust you, I must find another place to stay. I must know, now." He frowned at her, his hands clenched together before him on the table.

Tante Kees sat down. She understood. She reached across the table and laid her hands on his. "Eusi, I promise," she said softly, "we will not betray any of you, if we can possibly help it."

"Thank you, Tante Kees," he replied calmly. "I believe you and I trust you." As an afterthought, he added in a gentle voice, "But you should tell your sister to start really reading her Bible."

Later that evening as some of us rehashed the discussion, Leendert observed that perhaps Tante Kees' preparation for a Gestapo raid needed improvement. "Let me take care of that," he said.

Several hours later, in the middle of the night, he

tiptoed into Tante Kees' bedroom and shook her awake rudely.

"How many Jews have you hidden here?" he shouted at her.

"Four," she answered, before she was fully awake. That really frightened us, and on top of that the number was an exaggeration.

"We'll have to work at this," we told her.

She agreed. "You must do this again. I must get my reactions right." So we tested her many times until she managed to wake up with a convincing performance of indignant innocence.

We also hit upon another warning sign. Opa was an agent of ALPINA watches, so we put the glass sign which advertised these watches in the window of the living room. All regular visitors to the BéJé, seeing the blue-colored, triangular plaque, would know that it was safe to call. It's absence would mean: "Stay away!"

Many Dutch Christians faced radical changes in those summer months in 1943. Until then, lying, stealing, killing, and blackmailing were crimes before God and before Dutch society. But a demonic regime had taken hold of our country and our civilization, and we had to choose: follow their evil directives or suffer the consequences; help those in need or stand disinterestedly on the sidelines. However long one tried to avoid a choice, to postpone a decision, the moment of truth would finally come.

A government worker, for example, might be told to provide files or city records, listing all young men of a certain age group. The Gestapo would then use that information to arrest and deport them. To refuse to provide the list would mean a grave risk for the worker and, perhaps, his family as well. What's more, someone else would soon take that worker's place and, very likely, would obey the orders willingly.

All students and military personnel had to report for deportation to labor camps. If they didn't show up, the Nazi's might come and arrest the family. If they tried to hide to escape arrest, they put someone else at risk.

All across the country, the Germans posted "No Jews" signs. So should one continue to use public libraries, parks, and streetcars as if nothing was the matter? By doing that one would implicitly condone the Nazi discrimination and denial of basic rights to a group of Dutch citizens.

Then there was the forbidden radio we listened to each day. Should we comply or not?

With each of these we had to ask: If caught, do we lie? If we need food coupons, do we steal ration cards? Should we accept stolen ration cards? Is it right to kill to survive? What about living under a false identity? Isn't that living a lie?

I pondered these questions, wondering how to reconcile them with the call of Jesus to seek first the Kingdom of God and His righteousness. Gradually it dawned on me that the moment might be close at hand when I would have to decide whether to obey God or man.

LIVING IN TWILIGHT
5

It was almost midnight, and for an hour, we had been helping Leendert. He taught math at a high school, and the four of us had been checking the answers on a written test he had given his classes. We all heard the noise at once. A car stopped outside and men began to speak loudly, in German. That was all we needed. One of us snapped off the light in the bedroom, and we rushed into the emergency drill. I lay nearest to the door, so with my night bag in hand, I ran along the corridor to the girls' rooms and knocked, softly but urgently. "Alarm! Germans around!" I warned, and I heard immediate action.

The commotion had already awakened Tante Kees. She stood ready next to the entry to the hiding place.

I told her quickly what we'd seen, then slid into the Angels' Den. Henk followed within seconds, then the others. Mary was the last to enter. We dropped the panel and Tante Kees put the sewing boxes in their place at the bottom of the closet. The routine had worked. We settled in then, knowing we might be in for a long siege. At one point we heard steps going from room to room and guessed it was Tante Kees warning the family and checking for things we left behind. Still, no doorbell sounded. So we waited.

We had been there a half hour or more when we heard steps approaching, then knocks against the secret panel and Tante Kees' voice: "It's a German army truck, apparently with engine trouble. I watched them through a slit in the blackout sheet from the window in the parlor. But you must stay inside till they are gone, just to be safe." We agreed and settled down for a prolonged wait.

The major tension was gone, however, and about 2:00 a.m. the truck was towed away and quiet was restored to the Barteljorisstraat. Half an hour later we were all in bed again. It was a useful experience, and four days later, on July 9, we knew how useful.

There was a lot of German activity in town that day. Army vehicles drove back and forth past the shop, and Henny kept a special lookout while we spent most of the day on the upper floor. Toward evening our underground channels brought us the news: the Germans were planning mass arrests over the weekend. We could hardly believe it. Never before had mass arrests been preceded by such open activity. Besides, raids outside Amsterdam were carried out almost exclusively by the Gestapo. The trucks passing our windows and the soldiers marching through the street were obviously all German army. But it was better to be safe than very sorry. So by common consent we decided to sit guard throughout the night.

Henk, Leendert, and I took turns, two-and-half hours at a time, from 11:30 p.m. until morning. We excused Eusi because his Sabbath had begun; we didn't want to ask more from him than necessary. Instead, he slept in the Angels' Den, ready to help us in case of an emergency. Leendert woke me at 4:30 for my turn at the window in the parlor, and the first hour of my watch passed uneventfully.

Daybreak came, Saturday, July 10, and the streets were empty.

Towards 5:30, however, several groups of Germans on motorbikes passed, heading for the Grote Markt around the corner. They seemed ready for action, camouflage and all, and shortly afterwards a number of patrol cars followed, machine guns ready. Suddenly I recognized the uniforms of the Gestapo on motorcycles with sidecars. That was all I needed. Within one minute I had awakened everyone and warned them and was back at the window. From what I could tell the activity still seemed centered at the Grote Markt. There were no patrols in the Barteljorisstraat or in the Schoutensteeg, so we saw no need to hide yet, but we were all ready for the emergency alert. Tense, with nerves taut, we waited as the time crept by. The activity outside began to attract attention. Curious neighbors ventured outside, mingling and speculating on the cause.

Tante Bep served us a quick breakfast, and towards 8:00 we saw Henny, the shop girl, hurrying toward us on her bike. She turned into the side alley, and before she could ring the bell, Tante Kees opened the door.

"Invasion," Henny yelled. "Invasion in Italy!"

We were stunned, and for a few seconds we just looked at each other, speechless.

"Invasion!" we finally echoed. "Invasion! It's the beginning of the end!" The tension exploded into cheers of relief. We danced and shouted for joy.

I grabbed Mary by the shoulders. "Did you hear that, Mary? Invasion in Italy! They'll be free first. Now there's your future, right around the corner."

I had never seen Mary's eyes so bright and happy. "I can't believe it! I can't believe it!" she kept saying. Tante Kees, with some difficulty, got her noisy crowd under control again.

"I'll go upstairs and listen to the morning news. Then we'll know more details. In the meantime please, please keep quiet," she pleaded, "or you'll attract the attention of people in the street or the customers in the shop."

Several of us followed her upstairs to hear the good news first hand. But when it came, in a triumphant BBC news bulletin, it was a disappointment. It was not Italy but Sicily, not a powerful stab at the heart of fascism, but a cautious step forward from the African continent. Gradually, during the day as more news came in, some of our original optimism returned. Rumors about mutiny among groups of German soldiers in Poland and the Netherlands kindled the hope that this invasion might speed up the breakdown of the German-Italian forces. And the progress of the Allied forces in Sicily was promising.

Through the next days we took turns at the radio, following the Allied progress. We still sat guard during the night for some time, uncertain how the Germans around us would react. But now Tante Kees brought the radio downstairs and allowed us to listen during our watches. So when Leendert woke me at 3:00 for my turn, he passed on the latest news. It was quiet outside and, alone in the parlor, I listened eagerly to the 3:20 news bulletin. And I urged the Allies on in prayer, *O Lord, fight their battle and deliver us.* When I woke Eusi at dawn, I, in turn, passed on the latest news like a relay baton of hope.

Leendert provided us with our major activity that July. As a teacher at one of the Haarlem high schools, he had an *Ausweis* and was free to teach his classes and to move around. His hobby was Dutch literature, and several evenings in June he lectured to us on highlights of prose and verse.

One evening the van Woerden daughters, Cockie and Aty, were visiting, and a lively discussion was going on when Leendert came in, his normal enthusiastic self.

"Look what I've got! " he exclaimed, waving a small printed booklet. "Remember, I told you about the traveling groups of players in the Middle Ages? How they performed their 'miracle plays' in which God had to justify Himself because of all the misery and suffering in His creation? Well, a Dutch poet has now written a modern-day allegory, picturing the devil accusing the Almighty of allowing mankind to vandalize His creation. The devil also charges God with applying double standards: justice for rebelling angels and forgiving love for rebelling man. It's great!" he exclaimed as he put the booklet on the table. "Masscheroen 1941" I read on the cover. I remembered the name. The devil was called Masscheroen in medieval times.

"Why don't you read it for us one of these evenings, Leendert?" Tante Kees suggested. She picked up the booklet and leafed through it.

"Ah, I expected you to ask that!" Leendert answered. "But I have a better suggestion. Why don't we act out this poem? Those medieval players didn't need much room. We can do it right here!"

A storm of enthusiastic support greeted his proposal. When she could make herself heard, Tante Kees said, "That sounds super, Leendert. We can ask some good friends to attend. How much time do you think you'd need to prepare?"

"Oh, about two weeks, I guess," Leendert replied. "We'll have to learn the parts and we'll have to rehearse. And, of course, we'll have to set the stage. We must have four men's parts, so the four of us can take care of that. Then we need one or two girls in it, to act the angels' parts."

"Oh, Leendert, couldn't the two of us take those parts?" Aty van Woerden asked, all enthusiasm.

Leendert, mollified by such charming support, readily agreed. "Yes indeed, you can help us out there."

It didn't occur to Leendert that Thea or Mary might want to take part. After all, they were an inherent part of our small community. But I found out later that evening that they indeed felt excluded and they were quite hurt.

Unfortunately Leendert didn't notice anything and he continued to distribute the tasks. "Hans, you must help by typing out the parts. We'll start rehearsing in a week."

But all the enthusiasm didn't impress or fool Opa a bit. He beckoned to Tante Kees and, when she sat down next to him, he said, "Child, will you make sure that all this will add to the glory of God? Otherwise, I will not have it in this house." Fortunately she was able to reassure him before long.

We used all our free time in those weeks to prepare. The alarms and the nights on guard because of the invasion of Sicily made little difference. Leendert was the producer, director, supervisor and main actor, all in one. The last three days before the performance, the parlor was a mess during the evenings, full of people, gadgets, wires and loose parts laying around. Though concerned for her precious property, Tante Bep nevertheless contributed some white sheets as background to the stage. Leendert, who was to play the part of the devil, borrowed a minister's black robe to add to the illusion. The part at the end where Jesus would explain God's infinite love for mankind would be said from behind the sheet. Eusi, of all persons, was quite willing to give his voice to Jesus' words. Regular rehearsing ironed out many initial flaws. A blown fuse was the only major thing that went wrong during the dress rehearsal.

The performance on July 14 was a success, mainly due to Leendert's drive and efforts. Several close friends and relatives of the ten Booms attended and applauded, and even Opa, many of the allusions beyond him, was satisfied. The main message of God's love and the Father's vigil for His prodigal son clearly had reached him. He used the opportunity to get Eusi to sit next to him after the play, and Opa involved him in a lively discussion.

When his bedtime came Opa proclaimed, "Children,

the message tonight was better than I could bring in my prayers. Let us thank the Lord for His love so great, and pray for our loved ones." No air-raid warnings or unexpected alerts disturbed us when we all went to bed late, at the end of a perfect evening.

For the next few days the BéJé was a madhouse. Several new guests arrived unexpectedly, and the ten Booms would not turn them away until they had a safe place to go. At one point we had eight refugees. Henk Wiedijk arrived, trying, like me, to escape from deportation to labor camps in Germany. His undercover name, de Lange (DeLong), was easily decided: he was six feet, four inches, but his size caused some concern. The beds were too short for him, so he slept on a mattress on the floor. We worried more about how he would cope with the small entrance to the hiding place, but, being a good sport, he subjected himself to rigorous exercise going through the motions of crawling in and out. His presence didn't increase the time it took us to disappear behind the sliding panel, but so many people in that small space was unacceptable for a long period. Fortunately, the crowded conditions eased up after a few days when several left for other safe havens.

People with such different backgrounds, thrown together under emotional stress, can be a happy crowd, but they can also be an explosive mixture. So we kept busy. Fortunately we had several creative members to whom busy-ness came naturally. During the day we each helped with the domestic chores, then we did our personal cleaning, washing, sewing, letter writing, reading, studying, etc. Eusi, in his disarming way, often found excuses for not doing his part of the chores. One Sunday evening he offered one of his best excuses to Tante Bep. He had asked to be exempted from household work on Saturdays, his Sabbath, and of course we respected that request. But when he tried to escape the dinner dish washing one Sunday, Tante Bep demanded an explanation.

"You know, Tante Bep," he said hypocritically, "I so much appreciate what you Christians do for your faith and how you try to minimize the need for work on Sundays. I want to show my respect for your attitude and, therefore, I would rather not work on Sunday, like you." Tante Bep laughed out loud and sent him upstairs. He had earned his evening off.

Many evenings in the parlor became relaxing oases, and we looked forward to them. Henk Wessels entertained us with magic tricks; Leendert explained modern Dutch literature; I talked about astronomy and the star patterns in the night sky.

Mary began to lecture us on Italian culture and was soon giving a course in Italian. Even Opa turned up, endearing everyone by bringing a small note pad and a pencil with him. However, Mary expected us to do some homework, and not all of us had the time or perseverance enough to continue. Mary also played the piano very well and had an excellent voice, so she often led us in singing, or she would sing solos: arias from operas or chorales from Schubert or Beethoven or Brahms, perhaps, or from Mendelssohn or Bach. Afterwards we'd sit with the room lit only by a few

dim lamps while she kept playing. And while we listened we'd forget for a few brief moments our actual
situation, and we'd dream of a world without fear. We
especially loved to hear Mary sing *Solveig's Lied*, a
solo from Grieg's *Peer Gynt,* in which Solveig, Peer's
love, reaches out to him, yearning and hoping. On
such musical evenings we could count on Eusi to ask
for specific hymns. With his strong voice and full
range he could rattle the window panes.

"Tone it down, Eusi," Tante Kees would urge him.
"Tone it down."

Eusi took a liking to the Dutch hymn *Wat de
toekomst brengen moge* (Whatever the Future May
Hold for Me). There was hardly a singsong evening
that he didn't open the hymnal at this point and beg
the piano player, "Now this one, please." In the words
he voiced his own ultimate trust: "I do not know what
the future holds for me, but I do know the Almighty
Who holds my future."

We especially enjoyed hearing him sing the
Hativkah, the universal Jewish hymn of hope, and in
such moments the deep gap between Jews and Christians was bridged. Together we praised the Almighty,
Lord of our lives.

Thea felt she had little to contribute. "Most of you
know so much and can perform so well. Why don't
you let me sit and just enjoy everything. Believe me,
such evenings do wonders for me," she protested
when we urged her to take part. "What can I do that
you all can't?"

But soon, practical and down-to-earth Thea was
teaching us first aid. Now and then she turned the parlor into an emergency ward for about an hour. She
demonstrated and supervised, and soon all of us were

trying out the various bandages and dressings. One day when I was trying hard to dress a finger, Thea tapped me on the shoulder and pointed to the Tantes. Tante Kees was lying on the couch. Tante Bep, who seldom took part, was trying to get a toggle bandage around her sister's arm, to stop the supposed arterial bleeding.

"Thea, please check to see if this is all right," she asked. We both laughed at her flushed but proud face. Thea, feeling no pulse in the lower arm, praised her. "Tante Bep, this is perfect." We couldn't tell who was more proud, the nurse or the novice.

We had gathered for lunch one day, the ten Boom family and six guests, when we heard scraping sounds against the alley window of the living room. A few seconds later a ladder appeared and on it a man with a bucket of water and a sponge and wash-leather. Apparently he could see the group through the lace curtains because he waved to us. It startled us badly. Such a large group around the table might give us away. Was he really a window cleaner? Or someone pretending to clean the windows? And if he was a window cleaner, would he tell what he had seen? And would the word get to the wrong person?

Thinking quickly, Eusi waved back at the window cleaner and said to us, "Just go on as though everything is normal. In a few moments we'll sing "Happy Birthday!" So with enthusiastic singing and hurrahs, we celebrated an impromptu birthday and the window-cleaner laughed and waved again.

In spite of the activity, we faced many hours of

loneliness, walled in, day in and day out, yearning for loved ones, uncertain about the future, frustrated by not being able to do something, anything. Our hope was fragile and was often no match for the grim reality of mass arrests, transports, and shootings. Rekindled by rumors of good news, it was soon drowned again in the menacing sound of marching boots.

When Peter van Woerden, Nollie's youngest son, visited on Sunday evenings, we knew we were in for a time of outstanding music. For an encore, he had composed a piece in which he blended the sounds of the German army marching towards the seashore singing their battle hymn, *Wir fahren gegen Engeland* (We Are Marching Against England), with the drone of approaching RAF aircraft, their dive into attack, and their return home, leaving nothing behind but the sound of waves lapping on the shore. We often asked him to play it in a vain attempt to imagine the victory that we all wanted so badly.

The crowded household offered little privacy, but, weather permitting, I often climbed to the small flat roof to escape. Here was a space about twenty feet long and seven feet wide where one could breathe free, fresh air and enjoy the sunshine. We had attached reed mats against the railing so our movements would not attract any unwelcome attention from the streets or from neighboring houses.

Often I went there to peel a bucket of potatoes, and, the job finished, I would lie on my back, watch the clouds sail by, and dream away. I yearned for freedom and for the wide-open skies and the soft late-afternoon light that slanted over the spacious Zeeuwse polders. How I wanted to see again the country roads with their rustling poplars, the fields with yellow blossoming coleseed, or the wheat that would now be browning towards the harvest at the end of August. I was also homesick for my love, so dear, yet so far out of reach. We yearned for a future together and yet we faced such an uncertain and grim tomorrow.

In the twilight hours, after dinner and dish washing, when the sky was darkening and the stars would slowly appear, some of us would quietly sit there and escape for a short time the prison of our shadowy existence. But more often than not, the air raid warnings would send us downstairs and back to earth.

One July evening we sat in the parlor while Mary played, singing softly the music of Mahler, Schubert, and Brahms. There was no heavy lefthand work, no strongly resonating chords, just the lightly floating tunes.

"Mary, would you mind singing that again? That was beautiful," Tante Bep asked, after Mary had finished one piece.

Mary complied, and later I asked her softly, "Could you sing *Solveig's Lied* again for us?"

"No, not now!" she snapped. She finished her playing with a few strong chords and quite unexpectedly stood up and left the room.

"What's up? Why did she stop?" Leendert asked. I was taken completely by surprise and couldn't explain it.

"Tante Kees, why don't you take over?" Eusi urged. But the mood was gone, much as Tante Kees tried.

As soon as possible I left the room and made for the

roof. I felt I had somehow overstepped a boundary. I was annoyed at myself for having broken up a delightful evening, but even more so because I didn't understand what I had done wrong.

The fresh air cooled me down, and before long I was thoroughly enjoying the scenery. The rooftops and chimneys stood out darkly against the starlit sky. I could barely make out the dark cross on the spire of the Roman Catholic Church at the Nieuwe Groenmarkt. The drone of aircraft engines became audible, and two searchlight beams flashed towards the southeast, pencils of light searching, intersecting, almost playful against the peaceful night sky. Everything was quiet, then suddenly the bell at the old Bavo church chimed 11:00 p.m.

As I leaned against the railing searching for constellations, I could easily see the Big Dipper and count seven Pleiads. And there was Orion. Four months before, my sweetheart and I had walked under the same Orion, oblivious to the outside world and its horrors, and planned our future together. Now it seemed an eternity ago and so unreal.

"Blast!" I mumbled when I heard steps on the stairs. "Why can't they leave me alone." Then I recognized the shadow that stepped out of the door onto the roof and I softened. It was Mary. She moved quietly towards the railing and leaned against it, next to me.

"Hans, I'm terribly sorry for being so rude to you," she said, "but I couldn't sing that song, I just couldn't."

"Oh, forget it," I said, awkwardly. I wasn't accustomed to adults apologizing to a 19-year-old. "I didn't understand why you reacted the way you did but I

figured there must have been more to it. It wasn't
like you."

My remark broke her reticence and suddenly the
story of her love poured out. She told me how she had
met a bright Italian, Antonio Sanzo, in the early
1930's, during one of her Roman holidays. He was on
his way up, seemed assured of a promising career at
the Banco di Roma. They became engaged but, in
1935, the *Duce,* concerned with the purity of the Italian race, outlawed all marriages between Italians
and Jews. Their attempts to separate and set each
other free failed, and absence had only made their
hearts grow fonder for each other.

They continued seeing each other in the irrational
hope that conditions would improve. Now it had been
a year since she had last heard from him. "I don't
know where he is, whether he is in the army or
whether he is even alive. Maybe it's too dangerous for
him to associate with a Jew. I don't know whether I
should try to get a message to him. Hans, I don't know
what to do. Sometimes I feel so desperate. And today
is the anniversary of our engagement," she said sadly.

I listened silently, now understanding. In her story,
Solveig had come alive, resigned, yet loving, yearning
for her love and hoping against insurmountable odds.
But I hardly knew what to say.

"My goodness, Mary, why didn't you tell us before?
Aren't we willing to share each other's sorrows as
well as our joys?"

"You're a dear, Hans, but what could you or anyone
else do?" she answered. "I figured, what's the use?"

"I don't know," I replied. "I don't have the answers
to your sorrows, Mary, but listen, why don't you write
a perfectly innocent letter to your sweetheart. At

71

least that will show him you are still alive. We could ask Kik ten Boom to mail it for you somewhere far away from Haarlem the next time he comes to visit. And you could sign it 'Marguerita d'Italia.' How about that?"

She smiled at the use of her pet name. "Do you really think that would work, Hans?" she asked excitedly.

"Well, why not?" I answered. "Just take care no one can trace it to you here."

"Thanks, Hans!" Mary laughed aloud. "I feel so much better already. See you tomorrow!"

How Long, O Lord?
6

As the long July days crept by, the war began to impose itself even more than it had already on our cramped and uncertain refuge. On the nineteenth we learned that friends of my parents had been arrested, together with nine Jews they sheltered. Apparently their address became too well-known and they were betrayed. We took it as a warning for us to be more careful.

Tante Kees kept assuring us that "angels are protecting this house," and we kept telling her that that didn't mean that we shouldn't ensure maximum security. We worried that she was careless and talked too much to outsiders. She insisted that she knew her friends well enough to trust them. Still, many had already lost their freedom through the indiscretion of "friends." Tante Bep, on the other hand, was much more cautious and talked about us with the family only.

The military air traffic picked up as the month went by, sometimes with as many as four air raids a day. We took it as a good sign that the Allies were closing in, but it also caused us some concern. We had heard that some of the bombs meant for the Fokker aircraft factory near the Amsterdam airport had hit houses, a church, and a school.

One sunny day we lay on the flat roof and watched a few fighter planes buzzing around the high-flying bomber squadrons. Suddenly, in the midst of what must have been an air battle, a German fighter plane exploded and came spiralling down. We all cheered, even while we watched the pilot bail out and parachute down.

Material support for us arrived through Mies' good offices: a sack of wheat and a crate of pears. More cheers!

Our hopes continued on their roller coaster ride when we heard that a giant convoy, some eighteen miles long, was on its way from the USA to Europe. With the Italian government and defense in disarray, the invasion seemed at hand. Every news bulletin carried inspiring new details. Squadrons of bombers passed overhead continually, searchlights stabbed the night sky, and the air raid warnings kept us awake.

One night we came together in the corridor on the top floor, all in our pajamas, and sat there for several hours. We listened to the drone of the aircraft while we cheerfully shared our hopes.

Henk Wessels and Leendert finally left our small group, and a Mr. de Vries arrived. Tante Kees knew little of his background, and we felt uneasy about him. The person who brought him had only a vague recommendation. When he was quite critical of the Allies and cynical about our government and war effort, we became suspicious. He could well be a member of the Dutch Nazi party or an undercover agent, for all we knew.

The others sent me to Tante Kees to ask her to try to get more definite information about him. Who is he? Where does he come from? Can he be trusted? We remained very tense while she went out to find contacts and inquire about him. We realized too well the consequences if he turned out to be an agent of the Gestapo. But she came back early in the evening with reassuring information: "He's all right, but they say he's an extremely critical person." We felt relieved and a bit guilty, so we tried to be as nice as possible to him. He turned out to be an excellent singer and violin player and soon fit in unexpectedly well.

To top all the emotions, we heard on the news that Mussolini stepped down and was succeeded by Badoglio. Mary couldn't believe it. She was quiet for some time, then went upstairs to have a good cry.

It didn't help that rumors flew and an assortment of people on the run suddenly came and as suddenly left.

One day we heard of impending Gestapo raids right in Haarlem. A large number of Gestapo and *Schalkhaarders* (a paramilitary group of pro-Nazi Dutch) had arrived. We decided to sit guard again behind the parlor windows, taking two-and-a-half hour shifts. That would give us at least some advance warning in case of an emergency.

A few days later Kik ten Boom and two friends turned up unexpectedly. An underground raid went sour and they had to run for their lives to escape arrest by the Gestapo. All the beds were now taken, so they slept on the floor in the parlor. In case of an alarm, they planned to escape through the top floor window onto the roof because the Angels' Den would be full.

The war came even closer when I learned that *Ausweise,* certificates of exemption, for all males born in 1923 and 1924 had become invalid. Several thousand young men about my age were arrested and deported to Germany. But almost at the same hour I learned that the underground had captured many new rations cards in successful raids on several distribution centers, and several complete citizens' record files disappeared in the cities of Soest, Apeldoorn, and Leeuwarden.

Inadvertently, it was de Vries who brought out the fears that lay uneasily and unspoken beneath the surface of daily conversation.

It began with a Bible study conducted one afternoon by Willem ten Boom. Eusi criticized his Christian interpretation of Old Testament texts and offered different interpretations current in Talmudic and general Jewish tradition. That didn't surprise us. Given the circumstances, it was inevitable that both sides would feel frustrated. Attempts by Tante Kees to smooth over the differences failed. When the Bible study was finished we went upstairs to the boys' room and Eusi sulked.

"See what I mean," he said. "Haven't I said this all along? This shows how dependent we are on Christian charity. We can't even stand up at such teaching and walk out of the room without appearing discourteous."

"Eusi, that's not fair," I retorted. "Nobody asked you to attend. And he's as entitled to his convictions as you are to yours."

"Ah, do you expect me to remain upstairs and keep quiet and not stand up for my tradition? And let you all be subjected to his views without hearing mine?" Eusi shot out, angrily.

Obviously he was too upset to be rational, yet I didn't give up. "At least they give you the freedom here to be yourself and to practice your faith," I told Eusi, "even if they don't agree with you. Surely the Huns wouldn't let you do that in their labor camps."

Eusi broke loose, "Ah, gratitude again . . ." But he broke off when he saw de Vries look at me in astonishment.

"What's the matter with you, Hans? Do you really believe that rubbish about labor camps?" The terse, clipped sentence mirrored his anger.

We normally avoided that topic. We all knew that arrested Jews were taken to a concentration camp at Westerbork in the eastern part of the country. From there, regularly, a train of cattle cars carried some two thousand prisoners with their few possessions off to the East. Some said they were going to Eastern Germany, some said to Poland. The Germans said they were headed for labor camps. Their all-out war effort required all able-bodied males at the fronts. Requisitioning replacement labor from occupied countries (not only Jews but also non-Jews) sounded

perfectly plausible. But in the last months we had
begun to have deeper concern over these transports
from Westerbork. Nobody knew exactly what was
happening in the East. No letters came from there
through the Red Cross, no acknowledgement of packages or messages sent ever returned—only death
notices now and then, with the cause of death listed
as pneumonia or the like. We all secretly feared the
worst, but nobody knew for sure.

Now de Vries opened the issue and the dam broke.
"Labor camps, my foot," he cried. "Don't you believe a
word of it. They are death camps to kill all Jews.
That's the truth. People have survived Buchenwald
and Dachau and have even returned from there. But
where they are taking the Jews now, nobody returns.
You're a crazy fool to believe what the Huns say.
Have you read *Mein Kampf*? Man, you yourself are
suffering from Hitler and you don't know what he's
after? It's all there, in black and white. We, dirty
Jews, have poisoned his Reich and its history. That's
what he says. We are parasites, and he hates us to
death. Yes, to death! He wants a pure race and clean
country. And therefore he wants to be rid of all Jewry.
He wants our influence wiped out. Listen to
Goebbels, his mouthpiece. He boasts that they will
now rid Europe of the Jewish problem."

He stopped, out of breath, and we sat there,
stunned. Deep in our hearts we felt that what de
Vries said might well be true, but we didn't want to
believe it. It was too ghastly to accept. Such demonic
ideas were beyond our comprehension. But we didn't
know how to react to his outburst.

Eusi broke the silence. "May the peace of the
Almighty— blessed be His name—be upon them. I'm

going downstairs to help the girls prepare dinner," he said, quite subdued now, and left the room.

I found a quiet moment to talk to Opa and told him about our discussion and our fears. Of course he couldn't give me an answer nor offer comfort, but he was deeply moved. Later, in our evening prayers, he brought all our fears before our Almighty Father in heaven, lifting our Jewish brothers and sisters up to His endless grace, pleading for His sustaining presence with them, wherever they were and whatever their fate.

Sleep that night eluded me. Deeply upset, I didn't know what or how to pray. I felt that I was involved, that somehow, sometime, the moment of personal decision was approaching, and there was nothing I could do to avoid it.

Each day of the long summer brought new stories of arrests of Jews in Amsterdam and arrests of people hiding. The tension built. We heard about regular transports of Jews to Poland, of mass arrests of all men eighteen and nineteen years old in the streets, of executions of arrested underground workers. *How long, O God,* I silently prayed, *can it go on? And how long before they find our hiding place?*

Then on Saturday, August 14, Nollie was arrested together with the Jewish girl she sheltered. Someone had said too much and the Gestapo got word. They knew exactly who to look for and where to look. They took Nollie to the Gestapo headquarters in Haarlem for questioning and sent the girl to the *Judenstelle,* the Department for Jewish Affairs, in Amsterdam. Fortunately, Nollie's husband, Flip, was on a biking

79

holiday. The maid, Marja, managed to escape through
a window at the back of the house and ran to the
BéJé to tell us what happened. Apparently the
Gestapo didn't know that Peter van Woerden was
around and he got away also. But the arrest brought
to an end a period of rare and wonderful intimacy, of
a unique sharing of apprehension, trust, and hope
among those in the ten Boom household.

From the moment we received the news we knew
we weren't safe and would soon have to leave. Tante
Kees locked the shop door and instructed Henny to
open it only to customers, after satisfying herself that
it was safe. We kept constant watch from the windows
upstairs, and we warned our resistance contacts to
"keep away for a few days, we have an outbreak of flu
here. Don't contact us."

Our main resistance contact, Herman Slurink, had
lived in the Dutch East Indies before the war, so I
tried to warn him in the Malay language, giving him
details and asking him to find out what he could.
After that no one was allowed to use the phone. All
through the weekend we took turns sitting guard
with two persons during the night. Now the girls also
took turns. Tante Kees and Tante Bep, between short
naps, provided food and drink, trying to relieve the
tension.

On Sunday a reliable Dutch policeman brought
news that Nollie had been interrogated, but he had
no information on what happened. Had she been
forced to say too much, endangering us all? Someone
else brought word that the underground might try to
liberate her because she knew too much and could be
a danger to many.

Monday morning brought mixed news. Nollie was

okay but had been taken again to Gestapo headquarters for further questioning that day. That meant a renewed and grave risk that she would be forced to give information which would lead to a raid. We gathered in the parlor, discussed these very real dangers, and, reluctantly, agreed that we had to leave. So during the morning the guests in the watchmaker's home disappeared one by one. Eusi went to good friends, the Jan Vermeer couple on the Schouwtjeslaan. Thea found temporary shelter with acquaintances. Henk went to the home of relatives. Mary and I went to my home. Others took our scant luggage so as not to attract any special attention to us and we all arrived safely at our new addresses.

Grandfather and the Tantes remained behind in a house eerily empty and silent. And while each of the refugees had difficulty adjusting to their new situation, remarkably enough, this was also true for the ten Booms. However quiet and safe their small household might have become again, when Mary visited them on Tuesday, the three of them independently told her they missed us terribly and wanted us to return as soon as possible. But though we heard no bad news about Nollie, we agreed it was still too risky.

In the next weeks Thea and Mary acted as couriers. They visited the various addresses during evening walks to carry news, messages, and requests. Eusi was restive. Used to company, he walked up and down his small room and bothered his hosts with all sorts of comments and questions. It was his way of relieving his tension and soothing his uncertainties. Thea was also unhappy in her new place. Her hosts hadn't wanted her to come and both parties remained distant, critical, and irritated. We had to find another place for her as soon as possible.

A week after Nollie's arrest we received more bad news. The Gestapo raided the home of the de Leeuw family on the Nieuwe Gracht, arresting them along with nineteen Jews they had sheltered. My parents and the ten Booms knew the de Leeuw family, and several of the Jews they had hidden knew Eusi very well. They might, we thought, know that he was hiding at the ten Boom's.

Bad news coming upon bad, we heard that Nollie had been taken to Amsterdam, but we didn't know if she had been taken to the prison or to the notorious Gestapo headquarters on the Euterpestraat. Stories of resistance workers who passed through Gestapo headquarters indicated that they would stop at nothing to break the silence of those arrested. They used mental and emotional pressure to extract information. They would mention, for example, "in confidence," a few well-known bits of information about resistance workers. Or they would promise to set the prisoner free in exchange for information. They threatened to arrest and molest wives, children, and parents. And they didn't hesitate to use physical torture to get what they wanted. We never knew who was strong enough or smart enough to resist or who would break and mention names and addresses.

The family was deeply worried about Nollie and depressed. Prayer offered the only solace. Everyone agreed that we should stay away from the BéJé, so the strange interlude continued. The ten Boom home showed the familiar quiet of a watchmaker's business, but its guests, dispersed around the city and longing for each others' company, managed to keep in touch.

Meanwhile, the war ground on. We heard rumors from many sources suggesting that the invasion was imminent. In a broadcast, the Queen told the country, "The hour of liberation is at hand!" We heard Churchill say, "I long for the day when the Allied forces will cross the channel . . . ."

This, unbelievably, was confirmed in the Nazi-controlled newspapers. But when would we be free? The waiting went on.

Early in September Allied forces began heavy bombing of Northern France and Belgium and even several strategic locations in the southwestern part of the Netherlands. The bombing interrupted the train service to Zeeland and the regular mail contact I had had with my fiancée, only adding to my agony. When Italy surrendered on September 8, the streets filled with smiling people, hoping that that turn of events would mark the beginning of the end of suffering for us, too.

On the day Mussolini was liberated in a daring swoop by German paratroopers (September 13), Nollie van Woerden came home, totally unexpected. Jubilant messengers from the BéJé brought us the news, and we could hardly believe it but we joined the ten Boom family in their excitement over her return. They showered her with hugs and kisses, and "welcome back" cards and flowers.

It turned out that the Jewish girl she sheltered was also saved. The underground raided the truck carrying her to Amsterdam and took all the prisoners by force from the SS guards. Of course Grandfather and Tante Bep and Tante Kees couldn't contain their joy. They continually praised the good Lord for His protection.

The real story of what happened and why Nollie

had been released never reached us. We didn't dare ask for details, and many questions remained unanswered. Nor did we want to spoil the happiness of Grandfather and his daughters. Thankfully, they agreed to our suggestions to play it safe and postpone our return to the BéJé for at least another week.

DAY OF DOOM
AND DESTRUCTION
7

The Jewish year 5704 was about to begin and we had heard warnings: "You'll see. The Huns will raid the hospitals and take away the Jews on their New Year's Day. They will make it a day of sorrow for the people."

It was Wednesday, September 29, 1943, and during the previous week, we had finally returned to the home of the ten Booms and the relative safety of the Angels' Den. Thea had found a new place to hide, but Mary, Eusi, Henk, and I were glad to be back with each other in familiar and trusted surroundings.

Even as we settled in, Tante Bep began to introduce a new addition to the group, but Eusi recognized her at

85

once and said, "Well, well, we wait for the Messiah and look who comes? Is this not the charming Mirjam, the daughter of my good friends?"

She smiled broadly. "Mister Mossel, I never expected to meet you in these circumstances. Now I feel at home with you around."

Eusi turned and with a wide sweep of his arm he said, "This is Mirjam de Jong, daughter of one of the most important men in our *mishpoche* (synagogue family) in Amsterdam. If the Almighty—bless His name—will bless you with old age, you will still say proudly, 'I have known Mirjam, the daughter of the great de Jong from Amsterdam.'"

"Hush, please don't talk such nonsense!" she interrupted, embarrassed. "I can better introduce myself."

Mirjam's parents, I learned, were still in Amsterdam. Because of his position, her father had, until now, been exempted from deportation, but following cautious advice, she disappeared while it was still possible. At eighteen years of age, she would not be able to provide the quiet stability of Thea, but in a few days she became a close part of the group.

Opa in particular enjoyed her cheerful chatter and loved to have her around. And she immediately took to the old patriarch and tried to assist him and to anticipate his needs. During evening prayers that first night he commended her and her family to our good Lord's keeping, and she whispered, "Thank you," and kissed him goodnight.

Since she was the daughter of an orthodox Jewish family, she allowed herself to be guided religiously by Eusi, and she quietly joined him in his daily prayers and ceremonial duties whenever possible.

She also helped good-naturedly with the domestic

chores. At evening in the parlor, she listened quietly to music, sitting on the carpet or leaning against Tante Bep's chair.

At daybreak the first bad news came: during the night, Henk Wessels' father was arrested by the Gestapo, together with a Jewish lady and her baby the Wessels had been sheltering. The Wessels were part of the same underground network as the ten Booms. They exchanged addresses, ration cards, etc., and that meant that our hiding place was unsafe again.

It was as if the Gestapo kept coming closer and closer. Again, good friends had fallen into their hands and were at their mercy, if they had any. Their future was probably hopeless and our grief was great. The arrested Jews would certainly be taken to the notorious camps in the East, and the members of the underground network would be submitted to ruthless interrogation. In turn, that interrogation might lead to the arrest of an entire group. We decided, reluctantly, that we had to disappear again and leave the family and house as innocently and inconspicuously as possible. But before lunch a second blow fell. During the previous evening and early morning, in massive raids, the Gestapo had rounded up all the Jews they could find in Amsterdam and had taken them to the railway station where cattle car trains took them directly to Poland.

Mary and I were in the kitchen with Tante Bep, preparing lunch, when we heard the messenger talking to Tante Kees. He also confirmed that Mirjam's parents had been among those arrested. We were stunned; this hit us personally. Tante Kees took control immediately. She cautioned us not to tell Mirjam the fate of her parents. We didn't understand why, but we promised not to tell. Then Tante Kees went upstairs and told the others about the mass arrests in Amsterdam. The shock was indescribable. Scores of relatives and friends of Eusi, Mary, and Mirjam were still in Amsterdam, their fates now unknown.

Eusi walked up and down the room, muttering and chanting softly, his hands lifted up in supplication to the Almighty for help and protection. Mirjam was extremely upset. Crying, she insisted that she needed to go to Amsterdam—now—to find out whether her parents had escaped. It was impossible to calm her down. Mary finally took her to her room where they both cried out their anxiety over their loved ones. But Mirjam still didn't know the truth.

Lunch was late and nobody spoke. Each one was alone in his or her own private agony. After lunch, Opa took his Bible and turned to Psalm 23. Mirjam sat next to him. He laid his old hand on her clenched fists and read the words of ultimate trust: "Even though I walk through the valley of the shadow of death, I will fear no evil, for You are with me." Mirjam began to cry again, softly. When Opa finished reading, he folded his hands over hers and prayed for us and with us, prayed as intensely and as involved as we had ever heard. "Trust, even in the valley of death, for He will not fail us, nor all those who put their ultimate confidence in Him," he prayed. We sat there numb, heads bowed, tears in our eyes, suffering, rebelling, desperate, outraged. "Into Thy Almighty hands, our Lord."

Eusi, Mary, and Mirjam went upstairs, and together they said the ritual prayers and dedicated their New Year to the Almighty. Then Eusi brought them downstairs to the living room.

"We have greeted our New Year together. Now we would like you to join us in our New Year's wish: "Next year in Jerusalem!"

The usually reticent Tante Bep responded first. It was as if she had waited for something like this. She stepped forward and we could hear her emotions breaking loose. "O, Eusi, if that could only be true! Let's pray for that, yes, next year in Jerusalem, Eusi!" Her eyes shone and she unexpectedly held him close and gave him a tight hug.

Then she turned to Mary and said, "Mary, love, next year in Jerusalem!" and she hugged her, too. By this time everyone had joined in, hugging and shaking hands, as if our hopes and gestures could make it come true.

Later in the day, after preparing for yet another departure, Mirjam helped me with the dishes. When we heard that Henk's mother also had been arrested, Mirjam, in spite of her own worries, commiserated, "And he does not yet know that his parents are in the hands of the Gestapo." Upset, I turned away from her. Here she was, her own parents gone, and she didn't know it yet. It had come close before, but never this close for me.

I had led a sheltered life and now I felt so helpless against such evil, such malignancy. I didn't know what to say, afraid that it would be only empty words. Suddenly my heart—not my mind—remembered. "Even in the valley of death." My feeling of helplessness receded and a deep-seated trust took over.

Quietly I started to talk to Mirjam about our uncertain future and that of our families. "You don't know where your parents are, and we don't know what will happen to us. You don't even know if you shall arrive safely at your new place, and I don't know whether I'll be arrested tonight. Everything is so insecure for us all. But remember what Opa read to us after lunch? We are never alone, Mirjam. Our God will be with us even in this valley of death. We do have to trust Him for we can't handle this ourselves anymore."

She nodded, her head bowed. In the living room Tante Bep overheard and came into the kitchen, smiling. She hugged Mirjam and put her arm around my shoulders. "Yes, my children, that's the answer. If you trust Him, God will be with you wherever you have to go, or wherever we have to go." Her faith shone through her pale features.

"Opa has always told us," she continued, "that God gives us more strength when the burdens grow greater. He'll carry us through on eagles' wings, if necessary, right into His arms." Her solemn words radiated the trust she felt as fact. "You will have to leave this home shortly, but go with Him." Tante Bep turned away, overcome with emotion. We had never known her to be so open and intimate with us. It was a gift from heaven at the right time and place.

That evening we vacated the BéJé again, leaving it strangely silent. Eusi again went to the Vermeers, while Mirjam went to the Minnema family in Heemstede, which we knew to be a center of resistance work. Before she left, though, Tante Kees told her the news about her parents' arrest. She listened calmly and then left the room to be alone. Tante Kees sent Mary up to Mirjam's room to comfort her, for Mary had suffered a similar loss. When Mirjam came down, ready to leave, she kissed everyone farewell until she ended up at Opa's shoulder, crying.

"God bless you, my child," he said, comforting her. It was the last we would see of Mirjam for the duration of the war. Mary and I left last to return to my parent's home.

That day I went through the depths of agony. I saw the fear of death in the eyes of my hunted friends, and I felt completely powerless to do anything. I silently blamed the Allies. They appeared to be fighting the war as though it was exclusively a matter of victory on the battlefield. But this war was different. Didn't they understand this? The demonic Nazi regime was ruthlessly destroying everything and everyone who didn't fit their goals or swear to their ideology. This war was becoming a battle against evil itself, not only against armed forces. Defenseless people, mothers, children, the elderly were persecuted and murdered.

Why didn't the British and the Americans bomb the Dutch railway centers at Amersfoort and Arnhem and, at least, stop the death transports to the East? Time and again I cried silently, "Why, O God, do You allow all this to happen? Why don't You do something?" But at the same time I realized that He would not come down and wipe out Nazism. Nazism could be defeated only by fighting it to death at the Allied lines of battle and through active resistance underground. That evening I realized I couldn't remain on the sidelines any longer. I had to do my part, no matter how insignificant it might be, to fight this evil.

For two uneasy weeks the BéJé was not considered safe enough for us to return. We heard conflicting messages about expected Gestapo raids in Haarlem, about the lack of progress of the Allied forces, and about mass arrests in Amsterdam again. Daily air raid warnings signalled continuing and intensifying Allied attacks on the German war industry. Rumors of an invasion increased.

Mary's birthday celebration on September 30 was sober, overshadowed by the bad news from Amsterdam. Our small but heartfelt presents of flowers, a bar of deluxe soap, and a copy of one of her favorite Italian novels (found in a secondhand bookshop) brightened her somber day somewhat.

The papers announced the execution of nineteen resistance workers as a Gestapo revenge for the murder of two of their henchmen, Seyffardt and Posthuma. Ten days later 140 resistance workers were shot, and throughout the Netherlands, churches held prayer services for those hundreds of arrested resistance workers whose fate was still in the hands of a merciless enemy.

The terror continued, however, with the Gestapo relentlessly probing every corner and possible hiding place. During a raid on a farm near Haarlem, some fifty Jews were arrested following a shoot-out in which van Duyn, a notorious police officer from Heemstede, was killed. We rejoiced because he had been a merciless hunter of Jews and students. But that brought even more Gestapo raids on a large scale all over the area and sent more resistance workers on the run. We heard that Mirjam had to move again because her host himself had to go into hiding. She went to the Dondorps', the family of a Dutch Reformed minister in Heemstede who was quite involved in underground work. We felt the incredible chaos all around us, like a small war within the main war.

The experience of those weeks profoundly affected our small band. Although only temporarily dispersed, we felt uprooted and felt a need to keep close contact with each other. We passed messages between hiding places and exchanged bits of news. We missed each other and the inspiring company of the ten Booms, the evenings in the parlor, and Opa's evening prayers.

The ten Booms felt the same way. Even Tante Bep came to visit us several times. We heard that when they visited Eusi at the Vermeer's, they had a vehement argument with him, and they told us they didn't want him to return to the BéJé. A week later, however, they had, apparently, made up their differences, and he was as welcome at their home as he had always been. It showed how tense and vulnerable all of us had become.

Saturday, October 9, was Yom Kippur, the Day of Atonement, one of the Jewish high holy days. It was a day of fasting and ceremonies for orthodox Jews. It didn't surprise me that Mary wanted to celebrate it with Eusi at the Vermeer home. She had come to the ten Boom home as a sophisticated nonpracticing Jewish lady, very much a part of the Dutch civilization. Like so many Jewish Dutch citizens, she was first and foremost Dutch, then Jewish way down the line. But gradually the Nazi atrocities and her personal fear and suffering broke down her self-confidence. The persecution of Jewish Dutch citizens made her increasingly aware of her Jewish descent and heritage. The more she related to the suffering of those

93

already deported or killed, the more she turned to the indestructible roots of Jewish tradition.

Eusi, with his unquestioning and unshakable Old Testament trust in the Almighty, embodied that tradition. By sharing with Eusi the purification and repentance before the Almighty Who had been the refuge of her people through the ages, she expressed in her way how dependent on His mercy she had become.

It was a process we were all going through, each in his or her own way. The raging gale broke us loose from our anchors of independence and self-assurance, and we searched, desperately, for sky hooks to hang on to.

CALL TO ARMS
8

In the final months of 1943, I was drawn more and more to resistance work. Since any young and able-bodied Dutchman had become fair game to the Gestapo, small local resistance units had sprung up and carried on a wide range of underground activities. Most of these began as rank amateurs but became professional in a remarkably short time.

Once I had made up my mind, I moved quietly to become part of a group. A friend arranged to have my identity card altered at an underground falsification center. They would change my birthdate and my occupation so I'd be less vulnerable to street arrests. As a 24-year-old assistant minister of the Haarlem Dutch Reformed church, with a certificate to prove it,

I would be, at least for the time being, exempt from deportation.

Tante Kees was jubilant. She jumped at the chance to be more involved, and she asked me to operate from the BéJé. When Pickwick came to our place to visit my father on some underground matters, I had a long and private talk with him. We discussed where I might fit in and the type of work for which he could use me. He mentioned courier work, transporting ration cards and messages, that sort of thing. So I settled down and waited for further developments.

In the middle of October, Mary, Eusi, and I returned to the BéJé. The days following were Jewish holidays, so we prevailed on Mary and Eusi to help out with household chores only when really necessary. Consequently, I was kept very busy. The mood in the house had changed. We missed Thea who had always been there at the right time and place, unobtrusively lending a hand unasked and defusing growing tempers.

I felt a growing lack of perspective, almost despair. The winter storms set in, and I knew that the good-weather opportunities for an invasion had passed. This meant another winter under Nazi oppression, another season of darkness, terror, and fear. And somehow the house had become more open, less secure.

Leendert, for example, came and went at his own pleasure. Tante Kees, charmed by his disarming and easygoing manner, didn't seem to mind, but the rest of us felt it was an unnecessary risk. More people came and went during the day or evening to bring messages, arrange underground matters, or just visit. One could hardly find a quiet place or some privacy anymore.

Several guests passed through, most of them staying only a short time, but each needed to be told the house routine, the instructions, and the exercise for the alarm drill every night. And each one came with his or her own set of problems.

Nel, who arrived the last week of October, stayed for several months. She was on the Gestapo wanted list, and her husband was in the hospital. From the start, however, she was an excellent companion. In spite of her slight build, she turned out to be quite strong and tenacious. She never hesitated to help when asked or even unasked, and she was always ready for a joke or some teasing. She was inconsolable when she inadvertently damaged a washbowl and didn't rest before she arranged, through the van Woerdens, for its replacement. She thought she was as rich as a queen when she was allotted the cubicle that Thea had occupied, and she invited us there, one by one, for a cup of tea and a chat. There was hardly enough space in it to turn around, but she was perfectly content.

Ronnie Gazan was another valuable addition to the group. When Leendert announced he wouldn't be needing shelter any more, the ten Booms decided they had room for another male. So Ronnie came, sporting a butterfly tie and pleasant manners. He immediately charmed Tantes Bep and Kees who gladly offered him semi-permanent shelter. Handsome, quiet, handy, and helpful, he fit in easily. He had been on the run since August, 1942, fourteen months already, and as a result, he had developed a patient attitude and took everything in stride. Ronnie could match Eusi in telling tall stories and Jewish jokes, and after the day's work, the five of us often gathered in the boys' room. In that small chamber we temporarily forgot the harsh reality outside and enjoyed each other's company.

The uncertainty of it all, however, stretched my nerves to the limit. With such a hopeless outlook, day after day, it didn't take too much to aggravate any of us. I longed for my new identity and the freedom it would give me to actively help my friends. And I yearned for Mies. Six event-filled months had gone by and our only contact was an infrequent letter. For security reasons I could only write about neutral subjects. I couldn't share with her the agony we had gone through, except in the most general terms. She was so preciously close to me, yet so painfully distant.

When I finally got a letter from her in October, I exploded. She was attending a teachers' college in Middelburg, and she wrote about the fun she had with her friends each day on the train ride to school. That completely innocent detail got to me. I could picture her in her disarming sweet-seventeen innocence, enjoying the freedom and fun that I certainly wanted her to enjoy to the full. Yet that same freedom was unattainable and impossible for me. Suddenly I became insanely jealous of all those young people, unknown to me but enjoying the pleasure of her company. I threw the letter on the bed and began pacing the room like a caged animal.

Just then Eusi barged in, and when he saw my rage he asked, "Hans, good friend, what's up?"

Poor soul, he then caught the brunt of my anger and frustration. When he heard as much as he wanted, he burst into laughter and stopped my litany in mid-sentence. Before I could turn my anger on him, he pushed me down on the bed and sat next to me.

"Now listen, my friend," he began, "let me tell you something. Here we are, safe and secure, while all around us relatives and friends are being arrested and killed. And you are furious because your sweetheart has fun? What's the matter with you? You must be insane!" It was a bucket of practical cold water and it cooled me down. Instantly I sensed how unreasonable I had been and I was embarrassed.

"It's not the fun that she has, but the freedom I want," I said lamely, trying to make a point.

"*Aggenebbish,* poor soul. Self-pity, my name is Hans." Eusi cut me short. Then he reminded me of the day he heard how badly his pregnant wife had been treated at her hiding address, and how, in her condition, she had to scrub and clean and do all kinds of dirty work. I had cheered him up that time.

"Show me your fiancée's picture," he ended abruptly. Admiringly he tapped the photo. "So this is your sweetheart? Where is your complaint? Gone! See?"

He was right. His down-to-earth logic defused my anger and I was ashamed of myself. I looked at her picture again and realized that my love for her was deepening beyond mere romance.

Meanwhile, more and more Dutchmen were drawn into the underground guerrilla warfare. Some performed small but important tasks such as distributing the underground news monthlies. Papers such as *Het Parool, de Waarheid, Je Maintiendrai, Vrij Nederland,* and *Trouw* gave us the real news. The latter was the voice of Christian resistance, and many families

99

received it in their mailboxes with surprising regularity, put there by an unknown messenger. They in turn passed it on to others, who passed it on to others, spreading the word ten to twenty fold. These underground papers called us to arms, and while many answered, many more remained on the sidelines. Millions of Dutch men and women wanted no part of it. Afraid for themselves or for their families, perhaps, or for their future, they remained indifferent.

With so many passing through and so many mouths to feed, the BéJé needed a steady source of ration cards and new places to send those seeking a place to hide. So it became inescapably part of the underground work. Tante Kees' was a natural for it and she thoroughly enjoyed it. She often left the details to me, and it gradually took up most of my day. Promising to find ration cards or a new address was one thing; delivering the goods on time was something else.

Providing and distributing new ration cards required the efforts and ingenuity of many underground workers. The cards were essential, but those who were hiding couldn't apply for them. So an underground group would raid a distribution center when new cards were ready to be handed out. Though terribly risky, such armed raids became quite frequent, and incredible numbers of ration cards were captured this way. That November, for instance, in the province of North Holland alone, raids yielded 317,000 new cards which were distributed to the hosts of those in hiding. Couriers carried the cards from town to town, running the risk of the unpredictable inspections which German patrols carried

The massive manhunts
Rotterdam, November 1944

Photo by C. Holzepfel, courtesy Rijke Instituut voor Oorlogs Documentatie (RIOD)

The Hunters

Grandfather Casper ten Boom

A stolen moment doing domestic chores on the sunlit roof
Mary, Leendert, Henk, Hans, Eusi, Thea (l-r)

Music in the parlor, with Mary at the piano, "de Vries" on violin

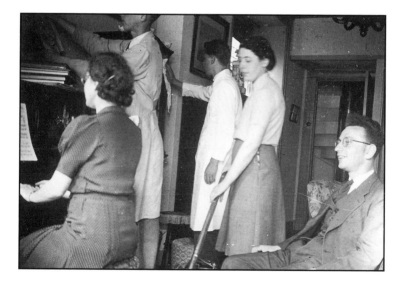

Saturday clean-up in the parlor,
with Eusi celebrating the Sabbath
Mary, Henk, Hans, Thea, Eusi (l-r)

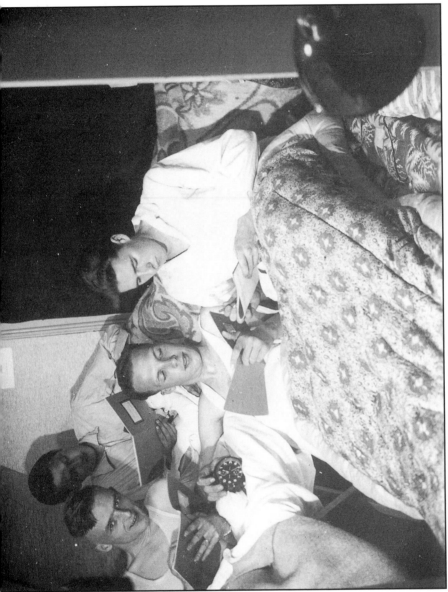

Bedtime in the boys' room

The ten Boom family with their "guests," September 1943
Front row: Henk Wiedyk, Mirjam, the father of Henk Wessels
2nd row: Opa, Hans, Mary
Standing: "Verdonck," Tante Kees, Mr. Ineke, Henny van
Dantzig, Tante Bep, Eusi

A peaceful Christmas in the parlor

Jan Hischemöller (piano), Hans, Mies, Tante Martha, unknown,
Henk Hischemöller, Eusi, Nel, unknown (l-r)

A wartime version of a medieval play,
christened "Masscheroen 1941"
Hans, Eusi, Leendert, Cockie and Aty van Woerden, Henk (l-r)

A formal picture taken by Haarlem photographer "Satina,"
July 1943
Front: Mary, Tante Bep, Opa, Tante Kees, Thea
Back: Henk Wiedyk, Leendert, Eusi, Henk Wessels, Hans (l-r)

Ausweis, stolen by the resistance

The dishwashing crew:
Tante Bep, "de Vries," Mary, Thea, Eusi, Henk (l-r)

Hiding practice: Mary exits while Thea helps her up

The house at Vredenhofstraat 23, Soest,
where Hans was arrested by the Gestapo

"Amersfoort"–a Gestapo concentration camp

Following his release from the concentration camp, Hans is
reunited with his fiancée, Mies

Free! May 5, 1945
Hans emerges (with hidden radio) from a secret hatch leading to
a hiding place under the living room floor in his home

From hate to hope: A welcome changing of the guard

The Hiding Place revisited—March 1974 Hans, Mies, Eusi and Dora on the flat roof of the Béjé once again

Reunion with Tante Kees:
Eusi, Tante Kees (Corrie ten Boom), Hans (l-r)

The ten Boom watch
shop, the Béjé,
Barteljorisstraat 19,
Haarlem

out on the roads and in the trains. With careful planning, however, the leaders often carried out their raids without shooting or killing.

With more and more people in hiding each month, the demand for ration cards and for reliable hiding places became greater. But the ruthless reprisals of the Gestapo against those who hid fugitives made many afraid to participate. Systematically, by torture or threats or through undercover agents who penetrated the resistance networks, the Gestapo found these hiding places.

And in simultaneous raids, they rounded up large groups of underground workers. These in turn became security risks, but others soon joined the ranks and filled in the gaps. The situation was developing into a full-size guerilla war.

Tante Kees had a spontaneous and inspiring approach to underground work, but her methods had serious disadvantages. Sometimes she changed her mind after a certain move was arranged, causing a lot more work for others. Sometimes she unexpectedly decided to include an extra appointment in a mission, upsetting the timing. But her cheerfulness and her honest effort to make a mission succeed made working with her a pleasure. Her carelessness, however, remained a continuing source of concern to us all. All too often she lost small notes which held addresses or numbers of required ration cards. We voiced our concerns to her in no uncertain terms and, time and again, she promised to do better.

Our underground contacts multiplied fast. The BéJé became a small part of a nation-wide network of Christian resistance, the *Landelijke Organisatie* or, as it became known, the L.O.

In mid-October, just after we returned to the BéJé,
I got a taste of what I might be in for: my father
miraculously escaped death. I knew he was active in
the underground. Sometimes he'd leave unexpectedly,
no explanations given, no questions asked. We didn't
know what he did or with whom he worked. But
apparently he was a key figure in the work of the
L.O. in his Haarlem district. District leaders in a
region usually met regularly in secret to plan and
prepare future actions in the region and to arrange
for future regional needs. Such meetings were called,
"The Exchange," and several times my father was
asked to represent his district, but he always refused
because he considered such large meetings of key
people an unnecessary risk.

On Wednesday, October 13, he was asked to attend
a meeting in Hoorn but again he refused to go. That
day the Gestapo, which had been quietly piecing
together bits of information, raided the meeting and
arrested those present. As far as we knew it meant
the firing squad for all of them. The number of
friends, acquaintances, and contacts we were losing
from our Dutch Reformed circle was growing fast and
dramatically. But still there was no end to the suffering. I was deeply grateful for my father's common
sense, but it brought home to me the extreme personal risk that my involvement in underground work
would entail.

While waiting, impatiently I confess, for my new
identity card, I busied myself with chores around the
BéJé.

One evening after a busy day, I went up to the
boys' room to write to Mies. Her birthday was coming
and with the postal service as bad as it had been over

the past months, I didn't want to risk being late. That afternoon Mary, with whom I shared many of my private thoughts and feelings, came to me and handed me a short letter in which she congratulated my sweetheart and asked me to include it in my own.

When I finished my letter I went downstairs where everyone had gathered in the living room. "What kept you so long?" Tante Kees asked. I explained what I had been doing, and she immediately exclaimed, "That's wonderful! I'd like to write her, too!"

I replied enthusiastically, "Oh, I'm sure she'll appreciate that," and I told her about Mary's note.

Tante Kees got out a note pad, and then Ronnie got hold of it. He wrote a short note and passed the pad to Tante Bep who quite willingly put in her share. By this time Opa had put on his glasses and was ready. "I also join in sending my sincerest congratulations," he wrote in a firm hand. And so the note pad was passed around the table, each of my friends adding his or her greetings. When he finished writing, Grandfather got up from his chair and left the room. A few minutes later he returned with a booklet.

"Here, my boy, send this to her, a small present from an old man to your fiancée."

He handed me a copy of a booklet he wrote in 1937, when the watch shop celebrated its 100th anniversary: *Herinneringen van een Oude Horlogemaker* (Memories of an Old Watchmaker). I was embarrassed, but delighted and touched, by the personal gesture of this precious grandfather whom I loved and respected so much. I didn't know how to thank him.

He waved away my attempts and said, simply, "We love you very much, so we love her, too, and this is my way of saying it."

uitnodiging voor de verlovings-
receptie te ontvangen.

Hartelijke groeten

van Tom [...] [...]

Beste Mies. Hartelijk geluk gewenst
met je verjaardag en 't in zeer gelukkig
jaar toegewenst! ('n vredesjaar!!) 't Is
jammer dat je 't hier niet eens eens
kunt. want 't is hier zo gezellig.
'k Hoop dat je 'n heerlijke dag zult
hebben en misschien kom je na
de oorlog hier ook wel eens kijken.
'k Hoop dat 't gauw is.
Vele groeten van de tante Bep (van Hans)

Ook ik feliciteer je hartelijk.

Opa ten Boom

Beste Mies
'k Verlang er naar je eens te leren kennen. Je hebt
een braaf[...] jongen, maar dat mag je hem niet
vertellen, dat ik dat schrijf. We houden allemaal erg veel
van hem. Hartelijk gefeliciteerd. God geve je veel
gezondheid en succes met je studie en vooral met de
Heerlijke zekerheid Jezus' eigendom te zijn.
'k Hartelijke groeten ze Tante Kees

English Translation

. . . and I'm looking forward to receiving an invitation to the formal engagement party!
Best wishes,
Tom van Sevenhuysen
[undercover name of Ronnie Gazan]

Dear Mies, I wish you a happy birthday and a blessed year (a year of peace!). It is so *gezellig* here, and we regret that you cannot drop in for a visit. I hope your birthday will be an enjoyable one. Maybe it will be possible for you to visit us after the war—which I hope will be soon.
Warmest greetings from Tante Bep (Hans')

I also join in sending my sincerest congratulations.
Opa ten Boom

Dear Mies,
I look forward to getting to know you. You have a very likable boyfriend, but don't tell him I wrote you so! We all love him very much. My best birthday wishes. God bless you with good health and at school, but especially with the wonderful assurance that you are Jesus' own.
Warmest greetings from your Tante Kees

It was a very special letter that went out to my sweetheart on her eighteenth birthday and an exceptionally bright moment among those long dark days.

On November 21, my identity card finally came back. It looked perfect to me. My year of birth had been changed to 1919 without the slightest sign of tampering. I could see no erasures, and it had the same type of lettering and the same shade of ink. I silently blessed and thanked God for the craftsmanship and the cooperation of all those involved in this masterpiece of forging and falsification.

My upbringing at home, in the Christian schools, and in church, had provided me with sufficient knowledge of the Reformed theological seminaries and their specific doctrines to pass a superficial examination if there should be an unexpected Gestapo identity check in the streets. I was, therefore, relatively free to move around, and Tante Kees immediately enlisted me for almost all the courier work at hand. Now fully in her confidence, I went out on missions for her. We both enjoyed every minute of it. After so many months of imprisonment, I was excited that I could move outside again, and I was especially excited that I could serve my country. There was so much to do.

I was immediately sent to take several score of ration cards to addresses in one of the suburbs of Haarlem. This was the first of many similar missions. During one of these missions, carried out on a day when there was a warning out for Gestapo checks all over town, I was fitted out in a girl's clothes, a scarf, and Tante Kees' bike.

It happened regularly that the ten Booms couldn't hide those who came to the house for shelter because it was too full. So I had to search for someplace else, then take them, often with their children and their scarce belongings, to a safer haven.

Sometimes I delivered messages to other Haarlem districts of the underground, warning them of expected Gestapo raids or passing on information such as the number of required rations cards. After some testing, I found a good spot to transact business. I would meet the anonymous messenger of the other district in the entrance corridor leading to the *Brouwershofje* (a small enclosure with houses for the aged). At the agreed time, we met there, checked our security passes against each other, did our business as quickly as possibly, and disappeared again into the maze of streets.

One afternoon the war came closer than ever to the BéJé. A British pilot whose plane had been shot down parachuted safely and the underground picked him up. When he came to the shop with his resistance contact, Henny immediately identified them as strangers and pressed the general alarm button.

We soon established their reliability, but Tante Kees was adamant: the pilot could not stay. She considered this too great a risk, a too active participation in the anti-German action. In a way she was right. Assisting pilots to escape was punishable by death, just as possessing a gun was punishable by death, most times without a formal trial. She wanted nothing to do with it and threw the responsibility to me.

As I'd done before, I turned to Pickwick, our trusted friend. He listened to our plight, then called back an hour later with specific instructions. Early in the evening, I walked, pushing the bike, with the pilot to the Oosterduinlaan in a suburb of Haarlem called, Aerdenhout. As Pickwick had indicated, I found a deserted tennis court and a small club house with the door unlocked, and I left the pilot there. He was to spend the night there, and someone would pick him up the next day and channel him into the pilots' lifeline through Belgium and France and, we hoped, on to freedom in Spain. As I cycled home, I thanked God for such competent help from underground friends. And I said a special prayer of thanks when this mission was completed without trouble.

The incident helped Tante Kees to see that she would draw the line at armed resistance. Sheltering and helping people was one thing, but she wouldn't be involved in more violent resistance. We appreciated her reasons for doing so and we respected her for it. As irrational as it seemed to me, she fully believed that as long as she sheltered and helped the hunted, she could count on the Lord to protect their home. "Angels stand guard around this house," she kept saying.

As I was drawn more and more into underground work, I received requests for help that included the use of weapons. Gradually, in addition to my work for Tante Kees, I became involved in more militant work. Neither Tante Kees nor my parents knew anything of this. When I was out, they assumed that it was on one of her missions, and, fortunately, they didn't ask questions.

Eventually my involvement deepened. It began

with fairly simple tasks such as staking out a notorious Haarlem Gestapo agent, logging his arrivals and departures, thereby establishing the route he took to and from Gestapo headquarters or the police station, etc. The resistance was considering his liquidation.

But I soon moved to tasks such as exploring the layout of a distribution center for new rations cards in a village north of Haarlem, in anticipation of a raid on that center. My superiors gave me a small handgun to use in emergencies, and without my parents knowing it, I hid it behind the books on one of the shelves in my room at home. Nobody would expect it there, I thought, let alone search for it. Still, all this remained a sideline. Most of the time I was busy with missions for Tante Kees.

The advent of Sinterklaas, the annual Dutch day and evening of gift giving and family fun, brought a special atmosphere to the BéJé. We decided we'd treat the ten Booms to some special gifts but not exchange gifts among ourselves. I was free to move around, so I bought the gifts. The others worked on poems or surprise packages to go with the gifts. For days, an atmosphere of secrecy pervaded the entire house. But the evening itself brought us the greatest surprise of all. The ten Boom family had a small present for each of us, and all of the guests had prepared gifts for each other; in spite of the gloomy outside circumstances, we had a hilarious evening. Down deep, we felt the power of close fellowship. We had been thrown together and were dependent on each other. And we treasured the gifts as tokens that told each other, "We love you!" And we all needed that.

A Gestapo raid the next day brought us back to reality. They raided the house of a Dutch Reformed minister, Rev. Siertsema, one of the more outspoken anti-Nazi ministers of our church. His house and family were a center of spiritual and active resistance, but under pressure during interrogation, two young men had mentioned the address.

When the Gestapo entered the house, Evert van Leyenhorst, who was engaged to the daughter, Bep Siertsema, happened to be there. Evert was heavily involved in resistance work, and, assuming the Gestapo were after him, he jumped from the second-floor window and fatally injured himself in the fall.

I was stunned when we heard the news late that Monday. I had met Evert several times in the course of my missions and I liked him. We had similar backgrounds and goals in life and we trusted each other. I was new to the work and I learned to rely on his experience and guidance. With his death I lost a valuable comrade-in-arms and friend.

The jubilee of the shopgirl, Henny van Dantzig, was a bright spot in those otherwise dark and dreary December days. She had worked for the ten Booms for twelve-and-a-half years and had become indispensable, tending the shop and its inventory and waiting on customers with her pleasant manners. In fact she was considered almost a member of the family. Henny didn't want any special attention that day, but the ten Booms insisted. She was asked to come at 9:00 a.m., rather than the usual 8:00, to give us time to prepare. Even Grandfather got up earlier than usual, and Cockie van Woerden arrived in time to represent Nollie's branch of the family. When Henny arrived we greeted her with *Lang zal ze leven* (Long May She Live), and Tante Bep welcomed her with a bouquet of chrysanthemums and an affectionate hug. Then Opa took over. He recalled the day she had arrived and recounted how they had come to love her and value her assistance, both in the shop and in the home. He presented her with a certificate of appreciation for twelve-and-a-half years of dedicated and competent service and with a personal gift.

Henny was visibly overcome when Opa hugged her. I know how much she loved the old man, so hearing him express his appreciation must have made her day even more special. After coffee and goodies, Tante Kees went downstairs to wait on customers and sent Henny home with the day off.

A Little Light
in the Dark
9

For a short period at the end of December, the evil outside the BéJé receded. The raids stopped and we saw little German activity. It gave us a wonderfully peaceful interlude for Hanukkah and Christmas, which came one upon another that year, and we decided we'd all celebrate them together as much as possible. On top of everything else, Mies was allowed to come to Haarlem for a few days during the holidays.

The time crept slowly as I waited for her impatiently at the train station in Haarlem. Finally the train thundered into the station, and we were together again and in each other's arms again. The months of loneliness fell away, and it was as if nothing had changed. We were together again. Was it the quiet before the storm, I wondered? No matter, I absorbed each minute of it and remember the details vividly.

Mies stayed at my parent's home, sharing a room with Paula Monsanto who was hiding there at the time, but she spent the days with me. We were oblivious to the world around us, almost too overcome for words.

I hardly had to introduce her at the BéJé.

"We've heard so much about you, we feel you're a part of our crowd already," Tante Kees told her.

Mary and Tante Bep busied themselves with dinner in the kitchen and several others, including Leendert and Piet Hartog, came by.

After dinner Mies explored the house, taking in every detail of the small world I lived in: the parlor with its large picture of grandfather, the sun clock, the heavy purple drapes. Then we explored the boys' room and the Angels' Den where I would sleep that night. It was a world hidden from evil, and it was where she would remember me in the months ahead.

We all worked together the next few days to prepare for the ceremonies and meals. Tante Bep dug up an old menorah for the Hanukkah festival, and Eusi told us about the tradition. Together we sang Hanukkah hymns, and their words echoed the fight for freedom in which both Jew and Gentile were engaged at the moment.

Together we kindled the Hanukkah candles, and whoever could make it attended the Christmas worship services on Saturday and Sunday. Those days were like a dream. We celebrated the festival of lights, the dedication of Jerusalem's Temple while there was darkness and evil outside, and the Jewish people were being led into captivity and being murdered.

We shared the good tidings, prayers, and hymns, and celebrated the coming of the Light into this dark world, singing about peace on earth, good will toward men, while a war raged about us, while so many loved ones were gone, and while we still lived in fear for our own lives. But we trusted the guiding hand of the Almighty, in whose keeping we were safe, while we walked in the shadow of death. God's light shone on us all, and it was comforting and inspiring.

Saturday evening we had our Christmas dinner. Tante Bep had saved coupons for weeks, and she let Mary take over the kitchen. In an unusual expression of appreciation, after dinner Opa loosened the napkin that was held by a slender silver chain around his neck, folded it carefully and, before getting his Bible, said to her, "That was delicious, and very special, my dear."

Later, after the dishes were cleared away and coffee was served in the parlor, Tante Kees read a Tolstoy story about the village cobbler Awdjewitsch. We sat around in chairs or on the floor and listened quietly to its message: Where love reigns, there is God. We decided for once that we would skip the evening news, and even Opa agreed that it would destroy our peace.

After the Christmas story, Mary played the piano. The music engulfed us in soft harmony with our dreams, and for a while we escaped the bitter reality outside.

The hours flew by too quickly, and Mies and I didn't have much privacy those days. We did manage to steal time away for a walk in the park, but then it was over and time for Mies to return to Zeeland. It was a bittersweet parting. She said farewell to her friends in the BéJé, and all wished her God speed with a cheerful, "See you next time in free Holland."

When we had kissed each other good-bye, I watched with very mixed emotions as the train pulled out of the station and her waving hand disappeared in the distance.

Neither of us knew what agonies awaited us, and little did we know she'd never see some of those friends again.

The peace of the season didn't last long. Strangely, it wasn't the Gestapo that caused a major disruption. It was the queen. On Friday, December 31, she spoke to the nation via Radio *Oranje*, encouraging us at the threshold of a new year. "Because of your attitude, and the courage and self-sacrifice of so many," she proclaimed, "this year will be remembered as one of the most glorious years of our nation. You have endured such unspeakable suffering and agony to create a nation that will prove that all the sacrifices have not been in vain."

Only a few of us had squeezed into the Angels' Den to hear the message, but later we all gathered in the parlor to discuss it. When Eusi asked, pointedly, "Did she mention my people?" we fell silent. The queen had made no reference whatever to the persecution and the endless suffering of the Jews in the Netherlands.

"No, Eusi," we acknowledged softly. Eusi stood up and asked to be excused.

"Eusi, Eusi," Tante Kees tried to keep him with us.

"Let him be, dear," Opa intervened. "I am deeply

disappointed myself." It was the closest I ever heard him come to criticizing our beloved queen. We were all embarrassed. Our government knew very well what was happening. So why this indifference?

As soon as I could, I slipped out of the room and upstairs and found Eusi sitting on his bed, his head in his hands. I sat down beside him, silently, only guessing what he was thinking and feeling.

"Eusi, we're so very sorry," I tried after a few minutes, and that broke his silence.

"Does it help me if you feel sorry? Does it help all those arrested and carried off and murdered if you feel sorry? Our queen talks of the courage of the resistance and our future government. Yes, those men are courageous, and I am grateful to them. They keep me alive. It is good of our queen to praise them. But did we choose to be hunted? Why not a word about us?

"And that underground paper, *Trouw*, that passes through here. What do they write about? Resistance, left, right, and center. But do they write about the Jews? Do they write about the arrests, the anguish, about the fear for one's life? Have we chosen to be persecuted? When they write about us they write about how many were arrested. That's all! But we're more than numbers. Hans, who cares about us?"

It was a cry from the depths of his soul. I put my hand on his knee for comfort, but I had no answer for his loneliness. I tried to assure him that we cared, deeply, about him and his family and people, and I reminded him of the song he sang to us about the future, when God would set them free:

Wipe away your tears,
give your crying a rest.

117

Redemption will come
at the Almighty's behest.

I urged him to come downstairs with me and let Opa pray for us all. He smiled, in spite of himself, and patted me on the back. But it took some time before he could face the others again.

That evening Opa read Psalms 90 and 91, the traditional psalms at the threshold of a new year, that contained a world of trust beyond worldly power. Then Opa prayed, interceding for all those, countless and nameless, who now suffered from the Nazi terror. He prayed for strength for those in the ultimate loneliness of facing death. He commended them, us, and all our loved ones to God's keeping, appealing to Him to make His presence remain with us throughout the year, and to take us under His wings, whatever might happen. It was a subdued but comforted group in the BéJé that huddled in hiding and greeted the Year of our Lord, 1944.

In those months the BéJé again began to get crowded. From nowhere, it seemed, two sisters, Meta and Paula Monsanto, arrived at our doorstep. While they were brought up as Lutherans in Surinam, a Dutch colony, they were also of Portuguese Jewish descent, and thus pursued by the Nazis.

A Dutch policeman had told them they were on the list to be picked up soon. Tante Kees, who knew them from church, had told them there would always be shelter for them at the BéJé. So they hastily packed a few basic belongings and suddenly appeared at the door in the alley. Somehow we managed. Meta, "Tante Martha" we called her because she was about the age of the ten Boom sisters, was a small, quiet, modest lady, helpful and kind. She shared an unshakable faith with the ten Booms, and she fit well into our small community. Even Eusi, for whom as a Christian Jew she was a renegade and even worse than a non-Jewish Christian, grudgingly admitted that he liked and respected that "Portegies." Meta's sister, Paula, was more outspoken and had much more difficulty accepting her loss of freedom. Meta, however, by far the oldest of the guests, soon became an example for us all because of her wisdom. When the atmosphere became unbearable and tempers flared, Meta's quiet intervention often defused what might have been an explosive situation.

January was hectic and full of minor frustrations. The activity of the underground network around us intensified and Tante Kees and I were drawn into it. Our now widely known shelter attracted those who desperately needed a place to stay or needed food or coupons or money. Although the house was overflowing, the ten Booms never turned away anyone who had no place else to go. Our own sources of reliable friends who could provide shelter had long been depleted, but new ones came regularly through our underground contacts. Every day, it seemed, I guided someone to a new hiding place.

Through the same underground contacts, ration cards with coupons for food and clothing, as well as money, flowed into the ten Boom house regularly. Tante Kees fully enjoyed her part in it, and I was so busy I had little time to think about it. I grew a small moustache to appear older and to fit my new birth date. I often delivered or picked up incriminating material and tried to be as inconspicuous as possible, and I took some part in armed resistance work. Because of an unforeseen shortage of ration cards, our group revived the plans for a raid on the distribution center north of Haarlem. We mapped out possible approaches, made dry runs, and explored escape routes. The tension built as we perfected the plans, but then, unexpectedly, the leaders called off the raid.

With so much of her time taken up by her involvement in underground work, Tante Kees didn't have much time or energy left for the guests in her own home. Often Tante Bep had to step in to keep matters in check and to arrange the details of our movements in the house. But she didn't have Tante Kees' easygoing approach, and relations became somewhat strained. Incidents that normally would have been forgotten as soon as they were over now became sources of continuing irritation and contributed to clashes later on. Meta and Mary attempted to keep the more emotional characters, Eusi and Paula, in check, but sometimes their efforts failed and tempers flared. Finally my parents took Paula into their home, but my father was immersed in resistance work so his home could hardly be considered safe. Nevertheless, they offered her hospitality, so Paula left the BéJé for the Lakenkoopersstraat.

Unfortunately this didn't bring us peace and harmony. One evening I came home from a mission to find myself in the middle of a shouting match in the boys' room. Tante Kees had received a warning from her neighbor across the street telling her that her guests could be seen from the outside, performing religious ceremonies. She rushed upstairs to the boys' room where Eusi, Mary, and Nel were saying their Sabbath prayers, interrupted them rudely, and told them to be more cautious. They responded indignantly that the curtains were closed, so who could have seen them?

Each party stubbornly maintained its position and emotions ran high. Finally Meta succeeded in calming everyone and bringing about an uneasy truce. But later that evening Eusi complained bitterly to me, "Hans, my *chawwer,* see? See how dependent we Jews are?"

Friday morning, January 14, began like any other, but suddenly Tante Kees called us all together.

"Get your things into the hiding place, quickly," she commanded, "and stay upstairs. And get ready to move at a moment's notice."

She had placed a call to her brother's home in Hilversum, right at the moment of a Gestapo raid. She hadn't identified herself and had quickly hung up. But she was afraid the Gestapo might follow up on the family connections. So we withdrew to the top floor and prepared for trouble. Was she reacting too strongly? Incoming telephone calls couldn't be traced. But it was better to be safe than sorry. Not until late that evening did we return to our normal routine, deeply grateful for only another false alarm. Apparently the Gestapo found nothing, and shortly after their raid, Willem came to the BéJé to visit his family.

During those hectic days, Opa maintained his quiet

stability. He still liked to discuss complicated watch repair work with his main repair assistant, Mr. Ineke. But most of the time, unperturbed by the busyness around him, he sat in his own chair in the living room next to the stove, reading or smoking one of his small cigars. Every now and then he would ask a question about the shop or the news or about his guests. He was quietly available to any of us who needed encouragement or comfort, and several times he asked me if Mies was well and if I had received a letter from her.

One afternoon Nel came through the living room, weeping softly, and went upstairs to the privacy of her room. A little later Opa asked me to go up and ask her to come to the parlor, which was unoccupied at the time. Opa was waiting for her there with his wisdom and his assurance, and at dinner Nel was her happy self again. "He is unbelievable," she confided later. "How I love that dear old man!"

When Eusi was upset one day, Opa read the Scriptures after dinner and asked Eusi if he would honor us by singing some of the traditional Dutch Jewish hymns about Jerusalem. As we listened to his great melodious voice, lamenting, yearning, and reaching out to our Almighty God in hope-against-reason, peace settled in our hearts and reigned again in our small community.

January brought joyful news to Eusi: his wife Dora gave birth to their third son. A friendly doctor had arranged a place in a maternity ward for her. When Eusi heard the news, it was difficult for him to contain his joy. He walked up and down the upper floor, singing praises, muttering Old Testament texts, and praying for blessings. Thus he welcomed this new-born and innocent Jewish boy into a hostile world.

Eusi couldn't visit his wife, of course, so he begged me to go. I hardly knew her, and I wasn't enthusiastic about the idea, but Tante Bep and Mary persuaded me. So I took flowers and blessings. I had to identify myself as a close relative before they would admit me to a large room with twelve young mothers, but fortunately I recognized Dora right away. She was radiant, so proud of her new son, and enjoying her time off to the fullest. By Jewish tradition it probably wasn't right to visit a mother so soon after child birth, but the Jewish laws didn't apply to a Gentile like me anyway. I reported all this to Eusi, yet he asked me the same questions over and over. They named the baby Joseph, or "Jopie," and soon we all inquired regularly about his well-being. Under the circumstances, however, he could not be circumcised and that bothered Eusi. His son would live for a time without the sign of the Covenant. But he was comforted by the hope and trust that one day Jopie would be part of God's future with His chosen people in a free world.

Meantime the war raged on around us. Frequent air raid alarms signalled Allied bombing raids on Germany and on strategic ports like Kiel. The news fuelled the rumors of an invasion at hand, in spite of the bad weather and the winter storms howling across the North Sea. One rumor was so specific we stocked extra food, fuel, and water in case of a shortage. And emotionally we prepared to welcome our Allied liberators. When nothing happened, it took another small chip off the block of hope we hung on to.

Toward the end of January, the Gestapo began to round up the remaining Christian Jews who up to now had been exempted from deportation. Meta and Paula blessed their decision to disappear while they could because many of their friends were arrested and taken away.

Finally, on Monday, January 31, I received an official paper from the Dutch Reformed church in Haarlem, stating that I was in their service as an assistant minister. With its official seals and signatures, together with my falsified identity papers, it made a convincing case for my new identity and profession. This backup made me feel more secure, and it helped me to go out with much more confidence. Little did I know how soon and how much I was going to need that backup.

He Sets the Captive Free

10

Saturday, February 5, 1944.

Hans, Hans, wake up! Put your clothes on and come downstairs." Tante Kees shook me from a deep sleep. "You have to go on an urgent mission. I'll prepare some tea and sandwiches for you while you get ready."

I followed her down the creaking stairs through the darkness, trying not to wake the others. While I gulped some tea and a sandwich in the living room, Tante Kees told me the details. A reliable policeman had brought a message in the middle of the night about a Gestapo raid. In the personal effects of a Mrs. van Asch, they found the address in Soest of a man

125

named "van Rijn." They had been looking for him, and they would arrest him early the next morning— unless I could get there first.

"You'd better take the first train to Amsterdam," Tante Kees counseled. "Now let's pray for your safe return." With our hands folded and heads close together, she asked for the Lord's protection on my mission.

I slipped out the side door into the cold and made my way to the station in the dark, trying to be as inconspicuous as possible. There was a 4:00 a.m. train to Amsterdam, and I hoped for an early connection to Soest. But there was nothing before 6:00 a.m., so it was daybreak before I arrived.

At the Soest station I saw two men in light raincoats who seemed to know their way around, so I asked for directions to the Vredenhofstraat. Fifteen minutes later I arrived at the house.

Hastily I rang the bell, several times to be certain I wakened them, and van Rijn, still in pajamas, opened the door.

"Who are you?" he asked. "What's the matter?"

In a few words I gave him the message and urged him to leave—immediately. There was a scene for a few minutes, with the man's wife crying and protesting, but I stressed again the need for urgency and then left. Mission accomplished, I thought. Now I need to get away. As I started down the drive, I noticed the two men in light raincoats, and I had a sinking feeling.

"Hold it right there!" one of the men ordered. "Gestapo! Who are you and what are you doing here so early on Saturday morning?"

Only moments before, van Rijn and I had hastily

agreed on a cover story, and I gave it a try. "I brought these people a message from their relatives in Amersfoort."

But it was useless. With a look of disbelief, they grabbed my arms, turned me around, and walked me back to the door. It took only a few short minutes for the Gestapo officers to search us, take our identity papers, and handcuff us. Sobbing, Mrs. van Rijn begged them to leave her husband alone. "He has a heart condition," she wailed. To make it worse, she admitted that I had come to warn them.

Before long I was on my way back to Haarlem, but now in the company of the Gestapo. My mind worked rapidly. I had to find a way out, a way in which I could explain everything as innocently as possible but, above all, without involving the ten Boom family.

In the train headed for Haarlem, one of the agents, Willemse, started to work on me. He told me I was a fool to involve myself in this type of work. He said he was not without influence at Gestapo headquarters in Haarlem. If I was willing to cooperate, he could use that influence to get me off lightly. The best way to cooperate would be tell the whole story, honestly, how I became involved, who had given me the message, etc.

"Moreover," he said jokingly, "as an associate minister you aren't supposed to lie."

But I didn't have my story ready and I needed more time. I hedged, "I have nothing to tell."

He laughed. "You'll certainly change that tune when we start working on you. But you better think twice, while I can still help you. When they get you at headquarters at the Nassauplein, I can't do anything more for you."

I kept silent, so he shrugged and gave up.

We arrived in Haarlem about noon, were marched directly to the police station, and put in separate cells. By now I was desperate. Even if I succeeded in steering my story clear of the ten Boom house, my own home in the Lakenkoopersstraat would surely be involved and ransacked. And there was that gun behind the books on one of the bookshelves in my room. That would be my undoing, or, most likely, I thought, my death sentence. I paced up and down my small cell, four paces up, four paces down, silently praying for whatever help I could get. The cell was actually not more than a short-stay holding room for drunks and petty criminals. Harder criminals were probably taken directly to the Haarlem prison. This temporary cell had a straw mattress, a stool, a folding table, and a container in which I could relieve myself.

Later in the afternoon I was taken to the headquarters at the Nassauplein, a notorious address in Haarlem where the local Gestapo extracted confessions by whatever means they could. During the short walk through the area so familiar to me, I was handcuffed to Willemse. They had taken my belt and shoe laces, so I walked rather awkwardly. It was Saturday afternoon and the streets were full of people who looked at us warily and then looked the other way. They didn't dare risk getting involved. When we crossed the Kruisstraat, I recognized a girl from church, and, startled, she recognized me. She looked as though she couldn't believe what she saw.

After checking into the building, we turned left and entered a spacious room on the first floor. A long table with chairs on both sides stood in the middle, and several filing cabinets stood along the walls.

Willemse's companion, Smit, was busy at the table.

"Ah, there's our preacher!" Smit exulted. "We're going to have an early Sunday worship this week. Let's hope he starts his service with singing so we can go home and get a good night's sleep."

"Not yet," Willemse said. "First let's compare what we have on him." He steered me by the arm through two open doors towards a large glassed-in veranda.

While he was handcuffing my left wrist to the central heating, I heard Smit say, "Oh, when I called to check on his identity papers, I found those idiots at the Citizens Register at City Hall had already left for the weekend."

Willemse grumbled something inaudible, shoved a straight-backed chair behind me, then closed the door behind him. It was impossible to hear what they were talking about, but the little I could hear cheered me up a bit. A check at the Register would certainly reveal that my date of birth was incorrect and show, in fact, that my identity card was altered. This in turn would betray my connection to the underground. So far, I was okay, but probably not for long.

After some discussion Willemse came to the veranda again, took me into the large room, and cuffed me to a chair in front of the table. Then they started their barrage of questions and threats. At first they were fairly quiet about it but, as time wore on, they became abusive and vicious. Amid the invectives I was asked the same questions over and over: Who was I? How did I receive the message? What was my underground address? Who were my contacts? What type of resistance work was I doing? For how long? And on and on!

By now I had a story ready but I tried to stall as

long as possible. Each hour gained meant an extra hour for all those who would by now have received word of my arrest. It would give the ten Booms, my parents, and certain resistance contacts an extra hour to disappear or to get rid of incriminating material. Silently I prayed that my answers would remain consistent. I maintained for more than an hour that I had left my own home that same morning and that I didn't have resistance contacts.

Then they switched on a strong light and adjusted it so that it shone directly into my face. The main light in the room was off, leaving the room dark except for the light beam that was now blinding me. I was hungry, and I was tiring fast from the emotions of the day and the endless effort to keep my thoughts clear and my answers short and, above all, consistent. The two Gestapo men started their furious interrogation again, but now they threatened me with violence and physical torture, and with the arrest of and retaliation against my relatives. Their questions and accusations tumbled over each other, flooding me with an intense pressure to yield. I was scared, literally scared to death, for fear of what might be in store for me and for others as well.

After a few hours of this, I felt it was time to jump into the unknown. Praying for guidance, I made a show of breaking down and I begged them to stop. Immediately they halted their interrogation, but the light remained focused on me. Little by little I told them the story I had made up, how I had a friend who I approached in December and had asked to get me involved, and how he promised he would. But I had had no further contact and had heard nothing until last night. Then at my own home I heard a short ring of the bell. I told them how I went downstairs without waking my parents, how I found an unsigned written message telling me to go and warn "van Rijn" of his expected arrest. I had burned the note in our living-room stove, I told them, and had gone, obeying the instructions.

Of course they immediately wanted the name of my resistance contact. I had a name ready: Evert van Leyenhorst. As they had hunted him to his death the past December, that would prove a dead-end street. But I was able to remain consistent with the story I had given them and gradually they seemed to realize that I could tell them nothing else. Finally they broke off the interrogation and switched off the light, leaving me completely exhausted.

"You do realize we're now going to your home to verify your story?" Smit said, with a sneer. I nodded. Willemse took me to the veranda and again handcuffed me to the central heating. They called in another Gestapo agent to do his work in the main room and at the same time guard me, and then they disappeared.

Thus began the darkest hours of my life. I knew that my parents' comments or story might expose mine as a set of lies. I knew for sure they would ransack our place to search for incriminating material. I knew they would find my gun, and I knew that would be the end, because possession of a gun in those days invariably meant the firing squad. I had come to the end of my possibilities. The shadow of death fell over me.

Everything that had been my life was fading before my eyes and heart: my love, my family, my future. Only one unshakable certainty remained: the promise of my Father in heaven that even in the valley of the shadow of death, He would be with me.

So I turned to God as I had never done before. "Lord, Father, here I am. You are my Almighty Father and I am Your child, but I have messed up everything and I'm so scared. Oh, please be with me, God!"

I saw no lightning nor heard thunder from heaven, but God answered my prayer. The handcuffs didn't fall off my wrist. But He gave me peace, indescribable peace, in my heart that told me: "I will be with you, whatever happens."

The peace that came over me conquered the other emotions—sheer terror and anger at myself—that were whirling inside. Whatever might happen now, I was His and in His hands, safe and secure. Nobody could hurt me anymore. I felt lifted out of my worries and agony and set up on a rock where no worldly power could reach me. I was untouchable. I was still cuffed to the central heating but I felt free, more free than I had ever felt before.

But before long I started to worry again. If my story didn't hold up—and it was highly unlikely it would—then others might be arrested and might suffer. I kept praying,"Please, God, make my story stand so others won't be involved."

The ordeal lasted for hours. Later in the evening the door of the main room was thrown open and a massive Gestapo officer entered the room, his overcoat open and his uniform with the insignia of rank and his decorations clearly visible. He was impressive and frightening. He reminded me of Rauter, the Gestapo high commander, and I was terrified. My guard jumped to attention. The newcomer asked him some questions, looked in my direction, then turned and left the room.

A few minutes later I had to relieve myself and my guard escorted me to the toilet. "Who was that officer?" I asked on the way back.

"Oh, that was Agema from Groningen," he answered. Gratefully I returned to the central heating. He had not come for me.

Late in the evening Willemse and Smit returned and so did my panic. They had gone to my home. What—worse yet, who—did they bring back with them? Neither of my parents was with them, thank God. But that didn't prove that they were in the clear. They might be in custody at the police station.

Willemse brought me into the room and told me to sit down.

"Well, you probably know what we found. And you also know what that means for you," Smit said.

This is it, I thought, this is the end. I grabbed on to the lifeline to my God, and prayed, "God, be with me, give me courage!"

Then Smit opened his briefcase and threw a few underground papers and a Boy Scout knife on the table. I could hardly believe my eyes. Was that all? Of course it meant prison or concentration camp, but they didn't find my gun!

(Later, after I returned from concentration camp, my parents told me that Willemse and Smit searched the greater part of the house and they ransacked my room, leaving it in an indescribable mess. My bookcase contained twenty-four shelves with books, and they had thrown the books off twenty-one of them, leaving three untouched. One of the untouched shelves hid my gun.)

133

Gratitude flooded through me. It was as if my God told me then and there, "I've given you a new lease on life, a new chance. From now on I want you to serve me, and I will be with you."

I tried to hide my elation and bowed my head. They accepted that as an admission of guilt.

"What your parents admitted to us corroborates your story. That makes it easier for us," Willemse said. He would never know how infinitely reassuring that remark was to me.

(Later my parents told me that Willemse and Smit, probably tired themselves and trying to get fast results, threatened them and had told them what I "confessed" and asked them if they could confirm it. My parents of course knew my situation and, hearing my story, realized it wouldn't incriminate others, so they were only too happy to confirm it.)

I knew then I'd be interrogated and harassed more about missing details, and I'd probably be confronted with other arrested resistance workers. But now I could try to answer them all within the framework of my trumped-up story. My parents apparently were off the hook and the ten Boom connection hadn't surfaced yet. Family and friends who were all so dear to me were not in direct danger at the moment. My God had blessed my story and protected us all for the time being.

"Let's call it a day," Smit said to Willemse. "God knows, it has been long enough. Let's get some sleep. We'll bring him over here again tomorrow afternoon, to tie up the loose ends. Take him back to his cell. I'll clear up the mess here."

Willemse hand-cuffed me again and took me outside. The clear winter air was infinitely refreshing after what I'd been through. I took a deep breath and fell in step with Willemse.

The corridor outside my cell had been quiet for some time. Then, late Sunday morning, I heard soft steps halt in front of my cell door, and I tensed up as fear gripped me. A voice said softly, "Hans, greetings from Tante Kees." I didn't answer. The greetings were repeated. I was uncertain, suspicious. It could be a Gestapo trap.

"I don't know who you are talking about," I said. The voice came back. "She asks whether she can do anything for you." I decided not to take the risk because my position was still so uncertain. "Ach, leave me alone!" I retorted, and that was the end of that.

That Sunday I was again taken to the Nassauplein, and Willemse and Smit tried again to catch inconsistencies in my story. Finally, it seemed they were satisfied with what they had on me, and I was taken back to my cell. That was the last I saw or heard of them. They closed their books on me and passed their reports on to the Gestapo for further processing and went on to further hunting.

Later in the day the same whispering voice contacted me again. Now the situation was different. I knew the Gestapo didn't know anything about the ten Boom setup. Moreover, the voice mentioned names and intimate details that only insiders would know. I told in a few sentences how I had fared, still careful not to indicate any underground relation to the ten Booms.

"Tell them not to worry about me. I'm OK, but ask

Grandfather to pray for me." I knew that I would be included in his evening prayers and that was infinitely reassuring.

In the days following my arrest I was kept in solitary confinement in a cell at the police station—alone with the beating of my heart. Those days I lived in emotional extremes—hoping, despairing, hoping again, despairing again. And I lived with the intense fear the Gestapo would find out what really happened.

Mies, I knew, was also at risk. They might then go after her in Zeeland and force her to tell them about my underground activities. I was frightened more for her than for myself, though I had no idea what the days ahead held for me.

All alone, the minutes seemed like hours and the hours like days. Still, I trusted the Lord's promises. I didn't have a Bible with me in that cell, so I relied on my memory for comfort from the Scriptures or for hymns to lift me from my misery. I thought often of Opa's prayers and the times they had helped me keep my eyes on the Lord. I took stock of my values and priorities, probably for the first time in my life, and I vowed I would try to live out God's love in my life and share my life and talents with others. Down deep, however, I still feared that others would suffer for my activities.

On Wednesday morning, to my relief, a guard threw open my cell door and announced I was being transported to prison. I still didn't know where, but I took it as a signal the Gestapo had closed my case and I could lay my fears to rest. I grabbed my few belongings and followed the guard outside to where a truck was waiting. I was on my way. That way would lead me eventually through prison and concentration camp where I would suffer hunger, pain, humiliation, exhaustion, diarrhea, and lice. I would be beaten, kicked, and abused, but I would never walk alone. God never left me. He sustained me and enabled me to survive and to help other prisoners. I knew now I was in His service.

WHILE ANGELS SLEPT

11

Commotion and anxiety reigned at the BéJé when I failed to return that morning. Once again those in hiding left for a seemingly safer place. All incriminating material was removed, and the house was restored to its supposedly innocent condition. Henny kept busy in the shop and Tante Kees worked behind her watchmaker's bench, along with Mr. Ineke. Grandfather sat quietly reading in the living room, and Tante Bep managed the kitchen, preparing meals or coffee.

Soon they heard from a reliable Dutch policeman that I had been brought to the police station, and when Sunday came without any calls from the Gestapo, Tante Kees approached her police contact and asked him to try to reach me.

A week or so later, the regulars returned to the BéJé. Eusi, Mary, Tante Martha, and Ronnie again became part of the ten Boom household, but they stayed upstairs most of the time, except to help with cleaning and cooking. By mid-February, however, the BéJé was back in full swing as a resistance center, albeit a special center with a clearly Christian heart to it.

One afternoon, for example, some resistance workers, including Arnold (whose real name was Reinoud Siertsema), a leader in the Haarlem-Noord region, met in the parlor. Suddenly, Tante Kees entered the room and interrupted their discussion. "Listen, we've run out of money," she told the startled workers. "There are some people here who need it desperately. Will you join me in praying for that money?"

The group wasn't used to solving problems that way, but Tante Kees, who relied on prayer for everything, insisted. So they folded their hands and closed their eyes, and, years later, Arnold still remembered that prayer. She reminded the Lord that they needed the money, yes, but that it wasn't for them but for His work on earth.

"We do this work as Your servants and in Your service," she prayed. "If we can't do it for lack of money, it is Your cause which suffers." Her prayers resonated with the psalms: "What profit is there in my death . . . will the dust praise Thee? There will be one soul less in this world to serve and praise You and, by the way, there aren't too many of us left."

The doorbell sounded during her prayer, and Tante Martha slipped out to answer it. When Tante Kees finished praying, Tante Martha re-entered the room waving an envelope with 500 guilders in it.

At first, Arnold thought, "Tante Kees, with your missionary zeal, you managed to pull that one off nicely, in front of the resistance workers and several who don't believe at all." Later he felt ashamed of his own lack of faith. "Why should her prayer not have been answered that way? When she prayed for the work of the Kingdom, believing God, was anything impossible?" Arnold reasoned, and he never forgot that vivid lesson in prayer.

The blow they had so long feared fell on Monday, February 28. It was a dreary Dutch day with business as usual, except that Tante Kees was in bed with a bad cold. About mid-morning Henny came up to her room and told her there was a customer in the shop who insisted on talking to her personally. Henny didn't know him and felt uncomfortable about him and told Tante Kees that.

Tante Kees struggled out of bed and into a house-coat and went downstairs to talk to the man in the watch repair shop. He told her a sad story of how his wife had been arrested in Alkmaar and how he could buy her freedom from a Dutch policeman for 600 guilders. He had no money at all, but people told him Miss ten Boom would be able to help him. When asked, he couldn't supply a single name as a reference to indicate that he could be trusted. There was ample cause for suspicion. Nevertheless, Tante Kees said she would try to find money for him, and she told him to come back late in the afternoon.

That afternoon the BéJé was crowded. Willem ten Boom conducted a Bible study and several outsiders also attended. A few resistance workers were there doing business, and the regulars were on the top floor, trying to stay out of the way. Sister Nollie and her son, Peter, had come to visit Grandfather. Nollie was busy with Tante Bep in the kitchen, and Peter was playing the piano in the parlor at about 5:00 p.m. when the customer from Alkmaar returned. Tante Kees came downstairs again and handed him the money. He left the shop and she went upstairs and back to bed. How was Tante Kees—trusting, compassionate Tante Kees—to know that the man was a Dutch Nazi working as an undercover agent for the Gestapo? A few minutes later he returned, accompanied by Gestapo agents. Henny saw them converging towards the house and suspected trouble, so she immediately pushed the alarm button which sounded throughout the house. Then she tried to block the men as they came in, but they easily shoved her aside. Still, if she had been less resolute, several more people would have been arrested.

Reacting instantaneously to the alarm, the four regulars raced towards the hiding place. Someone pushed Arnold and Hans, two of the resistance workers, up the stairs and into Tante Kees' bedroom. Sliding into the hiding place was routine for the regulars, and they were well on their way in when Arnold and Hans followed, a bit awkwardly, on hands and knees into the semi-darkness. The sliding panel swished down and a dry click indicated it had closed. Ronnie, who helped everyone in, checked it to make certain it was shut tight. It all took less than a minute while Tante Kees, now fully awake and anxious, waited for all six to disappear. She then threw her emergency bag on the bottom shelf, closed the door of the closet, threw off her housecoat and jumped back into bed.

But she had hardly pulled up the covers when she heard footsteps running up the stairs. One of the Gestapo agents threw the bedroom door open and shouted, "Who are you? Show me your identity card!" When she hesitated, he ordered her to get out of the bed. She complied and, standing there in her underwear, produced her identity card.

"Where's your secret room?" he demanded. And when she refused to tell him anything, he smiled, superior and confident. "Never mind. We know you have Jews hidden in this house and we'll get them. We'll search and turn this house inside out. We'll guard the house till we starve them out or till they turn into mummies." Her heart sank. He yelled down the staircase, "I've got another one here!" and ordered Tante Kees to go down.

She found the living room filled with people: Opa, Tante Bep, Willem, Nollie, Peter, Mr. Ineke, and Henny van Dantzig, as well as others who were there for the Bible study, all under arrest, faces to the wall. She also noticed in horror that the alarm signal, the triangular glass plaque advertising Alpine watches, was still standing in the alley window of the living room. Moving clumsily she managed to overturn the sign so that it fell to the floor and broke. But one of the Gestapo agents saw through the ruse. He pieced the sign together and put it back in the window. "It was a signal, wasn't it?" he said to her, not expecting an answer.

The trap remained open. For hours people kept arriving. Some came to warn the ten Booms. Some, like Grandfather's missionary friend, Las-schuit, came to visit and were snared, the innocent with the guilty.

Warnings also came over the phone, and the Gestapo gleefully intercepted them. Apparently they had conducted other raids at the same time, so they heard messages such as, "Uncle Herman has been arrested, please tell the family they may be in danger."

Meanwhile, Opa sat in his chair next to the stove, peaceful amid the tumult, as if it didn't concern him. Gestapo agents searched the entire house and soon discovered a small hiding place behind a board on the staircase. The valuables they found—ration cards, silver money which the family had saved, watches, and some possessions of Jewish families who were arrested or hiding—all disappeared into the pockets of the agents.

While the search was going on, the captain of the raiding squad took Tante Kees and Tante Bep to the repair shop separately and interrogated them forcefully. He ordered Tante Kees to take off her glasses and, after every question, slapped her face. She grew dizzy after the first blow, but he continued to slap her and she feared she wouldn't be able to endure it. Finally, she cried, "Lord Jesus, protect me!"

The captain shouted, "If you mention that name again, I'll kill you!" but he stopped beating her.

When Tante Bep returned, Nollie asked whether she too was beaten. "Yes," answered Tante Bep, "and I do so pity the man who beat me." When the captain continued to strike her, she also cried out, "Savior, oh Savior!"

He yelled at her, "Silence, don't you dare use that name again!" But again, he stopped abruptly and sent her back to the living room.

Toward 7:00 p.m. the Gestapo knew what they

were dealing with. They allowed some of the prisoners to go and relieve themselves, under supervision.
Those still standing with their faces to the wall were
allowed to take more comfortable positions. But they
allowed no talking. They sent Tante Bep to the
kitchen to prepare sandwiches but many were too
frightened to eat. When she came to Tante Kees, who
sat next to Opa, she pointed wordlessly to the mantel.
There, against the wall, stood a simple wooden sign
that said *Jezus is Overwinnaar,* Jesus is Victor. Opa
noticed her gesture and, following her glance, confirmed aloud, "Yes, we can be absolutely certain of
that."

Opa's statement prompted one of the Gestapo
agents to point to the Bible on the mantel and question the old man about the Christian's allegiance to
the government. "Tell me," he said, "what does it say
about the government?" Apparently he wanted Opa
to confirm Paul's statement to the church in Rome
that, "Everyone must submit himself to the governing
authorities." But Opa wasn't about to be caught.

"The Bible says, 'Fear God, honor the queen,'" he
answered, referring to the writings of Peter.

"That's not what your Bible says," the man reacted,
so Opa smiled and finished the argument.

"No, you're right. It says, 'honor the king,' but in
our case that's a queen."

Even in those ominous circumstances, he remained
his confident self. It was a bizarre conversation in
that setting, but somehow, apparently, Opa appealed
to some bit of humanity left in one of the agents who
said, "Old man, if you promise to behave yourself
from now on, we may leave you here."

To the surprise of no one who knew him, Opa

145

looked directly at the agent and replied clearly,
"Young man, if you leave me here today, tomorrow I
will open my door to anyone who needs help."

They looked at each other for a long moment—the
younger man arrogant from the power of handcuffs
and violence, the older man confident from the conviction of faith and knowledge of another power. And
the younger shrugged and turned away.

It was an unusually successful raid for the
Gestapo. They arrested some thirty persons at the
BéJé, and although no one knew what to expect, it
was almost a relief when, around 11:00 p.m., they
were herded outside. The ten Booms stayed close
together. Opa took his hat from the wall peg and
moved with difficulty. He leaned heavily on Tante
Kees' arm. As they came down the staircase he
noticed the large Frisian clock and instructed her,
"Don't forget to pull up the weights, dear." It was his
farewell to the home in which he had lived so long
and in which he had been blessed and been such a
blessing to others.

Handcuffed to each other, the prisoners walked
silently to the police station around the corner in the
Smedestraat, about a hundred steps away. In a large
room, normally used for physical exercise, they were
allowed to sit or lie on some mats or mattresses on
the floor. All their possessions were confiscated
except their clothes. A Gestapo officer sat behind a
writing desk at one end of the room and took basic
information from each one: name, address, age, occupation, relation to the ten Booms, their business at
the BéJé, etc. For two hours he wrote while two

146

policemen stayed in the room as guard.

Peter van Woerden noticed that the atmosphere in the big room was one of defeat and betrayal. He remembered how the family had often prayed for a watch of angels around the house and he wondered where the angels had been on that day.

It was the last time the ten Boom family would be together: Opa, his children and one grandson. One hundred years before, almost to the day, in 1844, his father had started a prayer group for "the peace of Jerusalem." And now here they were, arrested for *Judenhilfe,* helping Jewish people escape Nazi persecution and death.

There were others in the room also under arrest— Jews from other places and another watchmaker whom Opa knew. But was he reliable? They didn't know and they feared he was an undercover agent placed there to listen in on their conversations and gather incriminating evidence. With whispers they sent word around to deny any involvement in underground work. They had come to the ten Booms for Willem's Bible study. Thus they could restrict the damaging charge of resistance work and sheltering Jews to the ten Boom family living in the BéJé.

After everyone had given his personal information, they settled down for the night. But Opa, who apparently had regained some strength, asked one of the guards for the Bible that had been taken from Willem. Remarkably, the policeman complied, and Opa asked Willem to read Psalm 91.

The well-known words—with new meaning now— greatly reassured the group. The psalm promised the Lord's protection to those who trust and love Him. "I, the Almighty, will be with him in trouble, I will deliver him . . . ." When Willem finished, Grandfather prayed. His voice as calm and confident as ever, he asked the Lord to stay close to each of them, wherever they might be taken. It seemed he knew no fear, and through Opa's prayer, the Lord prepared the weary band of prisoners for an uncertain future. The Scripture and Opa's prayer changed the atmosphere from doom to quiet confidence that God would take care of everyone and everything.

The ten Boom sisters tried to make themselves as comfortable as possible. Tante Kees kept fussing around the family. She was restless and still quite feverish, but she was also deeply upset and rebellious. Tante Bep sat quietly next to her father. When she saw her sister's restlessness, Tante Bep tried to comfort her. The loving gesture caused Tante Kees to weep and to admit that her trust was shattered. They were doing the Lord's work. So where were the angels? Why had the Lord's protection failed? She had trusted Him so much.

It was Tante Bep's deep faith that weathered the storm that night. She reminded Tante Kees of God's protection of those who trust Him, not of their lives and physical well-being, but of their souls. She spoke about God's presence with them, "even in the deepest hell," and how He would give them courage for the new challenges they'd face in prison. Then she prayed for Tante Kees and for them all.

Tante Kees quieted down but, time and again her rebellion flared. Slowly, however, Tante Bep's faith opened the eyes of her heart, and later, while in solitary confinement in Scheveningen prison,

Tante Kees also experienced that closeness to the Lord, and finally entrusted herself completely to Him.

Meanwhile, however, they waited, not knowing what to expect. They were restless and sleepless through the remaining hours of the long night, talking little, whispering now and then. They agonized over those left behind and worried about how they'd handle unexpected situations. Some of those arrested weren't involved in underground work at all, but others were heavily involved and knew they were in deep trouble, headed for prison or concentration camp, or worse.

One of those was Henk van Riessen, who carried the code name "van Rijn" (no relation to the "van Rijn" I had been arrested with). He was a commander of the L.O., and early that evening he had received word that the Gestapo had raided the ten Boom house and were arresting everyone who came there. Knowing that his younger sister, one of his couriers, was due to meet someone at the BéJé that evening, he cycled as fast as he could to his parents' home, where she still lived, to warn her.

First, however, because his own home might now be in danger of a raid, he crammed his incriminating papers into his pockets, thinking they'd be safer with him in the streets than at his home. When he learned that his sister had already left for the BéJé, he pedaled there quickly, disregarding his own safety. It was dark when he arrived at the side entrance in the alley, and before he knew what was happening, he too was pulled into the trap and rushed up the stairs to join the others under arrest.

With all the incriminating papers in his pockets, he

had only one prayer: "God, don't let them find my papers," knowing it would mean certain death for many if they did. Never had he had such an instant answer to prayer. Almost everyone arrested had been thoroughly searched but, miraculously, he wasn't. The Gestapo agents questioned him, but he denied any knowledge of what was going on in the ten Boom house or that he had any business with them. He maintained that he had just been passing by when he was grabbed from his bike and taken inside. For a few moments when the guards left the room, he tried to stuff the papers into the burning stove, but just then one of the guards returned.

When they were finally taken to the police headquarters, he noticed how calm the ten Booms appeared, not at all frightened or worried, and he experienced a similar calm. What had happened had happened. Nothing could change that. Now each of them was on his own with only the assurance that the Lord was their Rock. That became his lasting memory of those hours: that one is really never alone; and that God heard his prayer.

At police headquarters, van Rijn asked permission to go to the toilet, and in the privacy of the small room, he stuffed the papers into the water but they almost clogged the bowl. To his surprise the policeman on guard outside the door asked him if he was able to get rid of everything. Apparently he understood what van Rijn was doing. When van Rijn came out, the policeman advised him to make sure he had nothing left in his pockets. Van Rijn checked again and found he had missed one small bit of paper—a skit on Hitler.

"Give it to me, quickly," the policeman urged, "and

I will throw it away for you."

Finally he was clean, his contacts were safe, and the Gestapo had nothing to prove against him. Deeply grateful to the Lord for his protection, he went back into the waiting room. Yes, he would probably go to prison, but he would go with a feeling of jubilation. He knew what was in store for him but now it would be easier to bear. However, Peter van Woerden was the next visitor to that toilet, and he faced a serious problem. Some of van Rijn's papers had surfaced and he had difficulty getting rid of them. He had to push them through several times to clear the passage and make sure nothing would resurface.

When morning broke, guards brought in rolls, and the group, hungry from their ordeal, gulped down the food. One never knew when the next meal would come. But there was no indication of what was ahead and no sign of their captors. An ominous quiet prevailed.

Toward noon, a Gestapo officer ordered them outside and onto a bus waiting in the Smedestraat. Many watched from the other side of the street, subdued and sad. When Opa appeared, supported by his two daughters, a murmur of compassion could be heard. He was so well known and loved in downtown Haarlem, and now he was leaving it, heavily guarded, like a dangerous criminal. Friends and neighbors wept as they watched the sorry parade. His daughters helped him mount the bus steps, and he slumped into a seat, obviously exhausted. Tante Kees took the seat next to him, and Tante Bep and Nollie found places nearby. To their dismay they suddenly saw Pickwick who had, apparently, also been arrested. He followed them onto the bus, his face bruised and swollen and dried blood smeared on his jaws, but he gave no sign of recognition when he passed them.

It was a pleasant and sunny day with a hint of an early spring. Tante Kees leaned over to Opa and put her arm around his shoulders and said, "Next time we see Haarlem, Father, it will be free."

Opa was too weary to respond but Tante Bep, who overheard the remark, said, "No, you'll see it before then."

When the bus left the downtown area and headed south, they felt some relief. It wouldn't be Amsterdam after all, not the dreaded Gestapo headquarters in the Euterpestraat. But where were they heading?

Opa's daughters talked with their father about the certainty of a future that was in God's hands.

"Whatever may come to pass, heaven awaits us," Tante Bep said.

"Yes, I am certain of that," Opa answered faintly but clearly.

After an hour's ride the bus reached the outskirts of the Hague, turned towards Scheveningen, and finally stopped at Gestapo headquarters. Tante Bep asked two of the guards to help Opa into the building and onto a chair in the hall. To their dismay, the prisoners recognized the Gestapo agents who had arrrested them. And when a guard said, "You might as well let the old man die at home," the agent in charge of the raid on the BéJé shouted, "That man is the worst of them all. He talks about nothing but Jesus and the queen."

Finally, after exhaustive questioning, they were

transported in a jolting old army truck to the notorious Scheveningen prison. So many resistance workers had been taken to this prison, and so many had left it for the firing squad, that it was called "Oranje Hotel," in honor of all those who suffered and died there during those appalling years.

Inside the prison, the group was assigned to cells, and Tante Bep, Tante Kees, and Nollie were separated from their old father. In spite of his physical weakness, he looked utterly tranquil. Tante Kees kissed him on the forehead and whispered, "The Lord be with you, Father," and he answered faintly, "And with you, my daughter." It was the last time they saw him.

When Peter, handcuffed to another prisoner, passed his grandfather, he stepped toward the old man and whispered, "I'm going to my cell now. Goodbye!"

Grandfather smiled at him and said, "God bless you, my boy. Aren't we a privileged family?" He was completely at peace.

Opa was taken to cell 401, which he shared with a man named Doris, a Christian Jew, and Henk and Simon, resistance workers. His striking patriarchal posture, his white beard and black suit, and the button indicating his knighthood of Oranje-Nassau drew their immediate respect. He carried a lump of bread, their daily ration, his mug, and his wooden cutlery. They quickly yielded a seat at the folding table to him, and one of the prisoners gave up the only bed in the cell. The others slept on mattresses on the floor.

Each prisoner also carried his own fear: the fear of the next interrogation, the fear of the next Gestapo attack on one's integrity and moral strength, the fear of pain and of ruthless torture. But Opa's mind appeared free from concerns for his own future. He was aware of the anguish and concerns of his cell mates, however, and he ministered to them lovingly, quoting the promises of God from the Bible and praying with them, especially when they were about to be interrogated. His unshakable faith became their strength and endurance. He also became their mediator when differences threatened the harmony they desperately needed. He bridged their disagreements and helped them to care for each other. And toward the end of the night, when steel doors clanked and prisoners were rounded up to be taken away, Opa carried that endless agony on the wings of his prayers.

By the following week, however, Opa's mind began to wander and his movements became vague. The brutality of prison life and malnutrition broke his fragile health. His mind and body gave out and his condition went quickly down. After persistent pleas for medical help from his cell mates, Opa was taken to the Ramar clinic, but he was unconscious by the time he arrived. There, on a stretcher in a corridor, entirely alone, God called His servant, Casper ten Boom, into His glory. It was Thursday, March 9, 1944. For Grandfather, the "best" had come.

Opa was buried in a nameless grave in a Loosduinen cemetery. Shortly after the war, the grave was identified and Opa was reburied. He now rests in the *Erebegraafplaats Loenen* (Gld), the war cemetery at Loenen, near Apeldoorn, along with hundreds of others who paid the highest price for their resistance to a demonic regime.

154

In the Shadow of His Wings

12

Back at the BéJé it was almost completely dark inside the Angels' Den and no one dared move. They heard shouting and commands and the shuffling of boots in Tante Kees' bedroom, and a Gestapo officer shouted at Tante Kees, "Sick? Nonsense! Get up and get downstairs, quick, quick!" After a few minutes, the sounds diminished, and a dreadful silence, except for occasional vague noises, pervaded the room.

Shivering, someone whispered, "Who's here?" The four regulars—Tante Martha, Mary, Eusi, and Ronnie—had made it, along with two resistance workers, Arnold and Hans. Arnold, leader of the Haarlem-Noord area of the L.O., had provided the ration cards for many at the BéJé. But the L.O. believed Tante Kees had become a dangerous contact, and Arnold had warned Tante Kees, "One of these days they'll get to you, and then you've had it."

"Arnold," she had answered sincerely, "angels protect this house."

But he had insisted irreverently, "Sure, Tante Kees, but one of these days one of the angels will take a little nap, and then it will be too late."

Arnold had arranged with Tante Kees not to come to the BéJé anymore. "You can get ration cards through a contact," he told her. "Write down what you need and put it in an envelope. Write a capital *A* on the top right-hand corner of the envelope and get it to one of our contacts in the neighborhood. Couriers will collect the envelope and deliver what you need to your home the next day."

But this was too time-consuming an approach for Tante Kees. So, on February 28, one of her messenger girls came straight to Arnold's home with the message, "We have some people from the region north of Amsterdam at the BéJé now. They need ration cards, so please come and bring some with you."

Arnold went there on his bike against his better judgment. He gave Tante Kees the ration cards, then went to the front room on the first floor to see if other underground workers were there. They liked to exchange information and underground publications. Someone might have the latest issue of *Je Maintiendrai* in exchange for a copy of *Trouw*.

Just after Arnold sat down, the door opened and someone shouted, "Beat it, all of you! Gestapo!" Arnold rushed up the winding staircase and into the small room where Tante Kees had returned to bed, sick. When she jumped up and held open the door of the closet for the others, Arnold dived into the small opening behind them. Once inside, he heard the panel slide down and the door close.

There were six people in that small space, without food or drink. It was a mess. Behind the false wall they heard the sound of the doorbell and the now too well-known code—three short rings and one long one—that identified a trusted underground contact. They knew those unsuspecting friends were walking right into the arms of the Gestapo. Later that evening they detected the sounds of a large group of people leaving through the alley.

In time they realized there was a guard in the house and that it was changed on a regular schedule. Each new shift searched the house again, determined, it seemed, to find the Jews they knew were hidden there. The tension in the hiding place was incredible, and it was impossible not to make some noise. Now and then they had to change positions to be as comfortable as possible under the circumstances. Some sat for a while, then stood to stretch when they became stiff. Ronnie had a cold and tried to smother the noise of his coughing in a blanket, but they were still afraid the guards would hear it.

The guards came upstairs often and searched, and each time those in the hiding place held their breath. They took turns sitting with their back pressed against the sliding panel, so there would be no difference in the sound when the guards knocked against the wall. They followed the chimes of the St. Bavo Church to count the hours that seemed to drag past ever so slowly. The men especially were hungry, but they had only a few crackers and no water at all. Before the raid the regulars had agreed to keep a supply of food and water in the hiding place at all times, but apparently, to their sorrow, they hadn't kept up with it. Because of cold and hunger and apprehension, sleep was impossible.

At one point, two guards came into Tante Kees' room, perhaps alerted by a noise. They knocked on all the walls and seemed to close in on the false wall. When they started to break up the floor boards, the hideaways thought, "This is the end for us."

But the construction of the false wall was perfect. The floorboards ended at the false wall, suggesting the outer wall of the house, and soon the guards replaced the boards and left.

In such moments of extreme tension, Eusi caused great concern to the others. When he began to pray half aloud in Hebrew, "I will trust in Adonai, who can harm me?" they silenced him with a pillow.

"Hush, Eusi! Your noise will betray us."

The situation became worse with each passing hour. They found a sheet, shredded it, and used it to urinate on so the fluid wouldn't soak down the walls. They used a small container with a cover to relieve themselves, but one night Ronnie kicked it over. He didn't have to tell anyone; the awful smell told it all.

After that the situation quickly became unbearable, but the quiet strength of those who truly lived their faith made the others turn to them. Tante Martha and Eusi both provided a source of new power with their assurances that, "If you trust the Almighty, He will be with you and He will protect your soul." Their confidence wasn't shallow, well-meant encouragement; it came from inner conviction, and they calmed the others in their anxiety and despair.

When Wednesday broke without any expectation of release, they realized that they might have to consider a breakout. The regulars knew the layout of the house and suggested an escape to the house next door. It would involve a three-foot jump from the flat roof into the gutter that separated both houses. But Arnold saw that the women couldn't make it, and he succeeded in postponing the escape. They finally agreed that if no rescue arrived before evening, they would go for it late that night. Arnold was convinced that help was being arranged from the outside and didn't like the risk their own action would entail. So they continued throughout the third day—hungry, thirsty, nervous, and afraid.

Meanwhile, Arnold's father, a minister of the Dutch Reformed church in Haarlem, chaired a church council meeting on Monday evening. During a break, he anxiously told a few trusted deacons, "Our son hasn't come back from a visit to the BéJé this afternoon." Providentially, one of those men was Mr. Hoek, the contractor who built the false wall. Immediately he told the worried father, "I know the ten Boom's house in detail because I built their hiding place. It will be very difficult for the Gestapo to find it."

So Pastor Siertsema went to the house of a reliable policeman, Jan Overzet, one of those who continued to help fugitives until they had to go into hiding themselves. Siertsema had often helped Overzet during those war years, and now the pastor himself needed help. Quietly, Overzet went to Inspector de Groot at the police station, a reliable officer who was in charge of the duty schedules for Dutch policemen. On the first day the Gestapo guarded the premises so he could arrange nothing. Tuesday evening, however, the Dutch police were told to take guard duty starting the following day. Normally this would have been carried out by unreliable policemen who were as bad and dangerous as the Gestapo itself.

Inspector de Groot, however, succeeded in changing the duty schedule in such a way that Jan Overzet and a colleague came on duty at the BéJé on Wednesday afternoon at 4:00. Hoek had given Overzet the blueprint of the wall, but even with that they couldn't find any evidence of the secret room in Tante Kees' bedroom.

In the hiding place the group heard the noise of footsteps approaching and then someone searching the place. Next they heard someone calling, "Siertsema, Siertsema!" Arnold felt like shouting for joy. Nobody could possibly know there might be a Siertsema in the hiding place except "one of us," because in the resistance he was known only by the code name of "Arnold."

"It's okay," he whispered as he pushed up the panel. Overzet put his head through the opening, but pulled it back immediately because the odor was so overpowering. The group came out one by one, staggering and dizzy and hardly believing they were being rescued. The policemen gave them water to relieve their terrible craving for something, anything liquid. Eusi was the first to get a swallow and began to praise God in a loud voice. "Sh, Eusi," they urged him, "Don't betray us after all this."

The policemen led the two resistance workers up the short staircase onto the flat roof, then into a gutter and through a skylight into the attic of the house next door. They managed to get to the ground floor unnoticed, then slip through the empty shop out to the street and on to freedom.

Then the policemen took the Jewish escapees to the parlor to wait until it was dark enough for the underground to take them to their new hiding places. The policemen stayed with them, guns ready in case unwanted visitors came. Around 7:00 p.m. they guided the four escapees down the staircase and through the side door and out into the alley. Resistance workers then led the four refugees safely to new shelters. A miracle had happened.

At the Mercy of the Nazis
13

When I boarded the truck outside the police station, I saw nine other prisoners, van Rijn among them, and I tried to talk to him, but a blow from the butt of a rifle made it clear that talking was not permitted. My worst fears were confirmed when we entered Amsterdam and the truck stopped in front of Gestapo headquarters on the Euterpestraat. I looked at the small windows of the basement, the place of torture, and a shiver ran down my spine. But I had no time to think about it. The guards jumped off the truck, rifles ready, and escorted us inside.

There—thank God for the Nazis' lack of insight—several large posters welcomed us. One was a picture of J.P. Coen, one of the founders of our overseas empire, with his motto, NEVER DESPAIR!, in large letters. Further down the corridor I saw a picture of the thoroughbred Aryan soldier with the caption, "As long as I'm alive, I will not give in." The Nazis had posted it to reassure their own colleagues, but, ironically, it provided unexpected encouragement to their victims.

After a glance at our papers, the guard at the desk remarked contemptuously, "Ha! All Jews!" and directed us to the section for Jewish Affairs. But on our way, a guard appeared unexpectedly and called my name. I stepped forward and was shoved into a large front room where a Gestapo officer sat behind a desk. Several stars revealed his rank.

"Are you Poley, assistant minister of the Dutch Reformed Church?"

"Yes," I lied, believing I needed to preserve this identity.

Then he began intense questioning: Was resistance work my way of preaching the gospel? Was the Reformed Church not proud of its strict acceptance of the Scriptures? Did I not know I was acting contrary to those Scriptures? Did not Romans 13 command me to obey the rulers God had placed over me?

I was astonished at his intimate knowledge of my background, but I soon learned he'd been a member of one of our congregations, which had excommunicated him because of his support of the Nazis. At a recent funeral, several old friends had even refused to shake his hand.

He jumped up from behind his desk and began pacing. "Here, this is my Bible now!" he shouted, and slapped a copy of *Mein Kampf* on his desk. He pointed to a picture of Adolf Hitler and bellowed, "There is my Führer. He is the only one I believe.

"You Dutch Reformed people with your resistance work, your aid to those Jewish lice, your distribution of underground papers, and your praying for a queen who betrayed you—you are undermining our new European order. You're preparing the regime of the anti-Christ. You're nailing Christ to the cross again."

He was working himself into hysteria and that worried me. "Oh, you Dutch Reformed!" he continued. "Two out of five brought in here for resistance work are your kind. And I know." Here he lowered his voice and leaned toward me. "I know we'll lose this war, thanks to your subversive activities. But then, mister assistant pastor, mind my words, you'll win this war, and on that day they'll hang me from that tree over there. But the day after that, mister assistant pastor, you'll hang from that other tree, next to mine. And my dead eyes will tell you then, I was right after all. The communists will be the ultimate victors. I'm telling you this today, and you'd better remember and repent, if you still want a chance to survive."

Spent from his rage, he dropped into his chair, sounded a bell on his desk and turned away from me. His words actually encouraged me, however, for they vindicated all our resistance efforts. When a guard took me to where the others were being registered, they looked at me, their questions visible on their faces, but I couldn't talk to explain.

From there the truck took us to the prison at Amstelveenscheweg where we handed over most of our personal possessions and received prison gear. Van Rijn and I were sent to the same cell, already occupied by three other people who surrounded us and barraged us with questions. "How is the war going?" "Has Rome indeed been liberated?" Then, after we satisfied them with what we knew, they went to the "prison phone" and passed the latest war news to the neighboring cells via the central heating pipes. We were each given a straw mattress with a cover and a place on the floor. The "seniors" were entitled to the three bunks.

Later in the afternoon the guards pushed a meal of four thin slices of bread through the small window in the steel door, and thus began weeks of gnawing hunger. I soon learned to drink a lot of water to avoid the misery of an empty stomach, and I learned the strict requirements of prison routine and how to avoid the harsh reprisals of the SD guards. It was only a place of transition, not my final destination, so I made the best of it. After the anxious days of solitary confinement, sharing a cell with several others was a mental relief. Having someone to talk to compensated for my hunger and for the badgering by the guards.

This part of the prison housed people arrested by the Gestapo for all sorts of reasons. Many of the young men had tried to escape forced labor in the German war industry. Some were resistance workers awaiting further interrogation or trial and sentencing. They accounted for the heavily armed guards and the many unexpected inspections. The continual departure and arrival of new cell mates meant we had to adjust continually to an amazing cast and variety of characters and to their reactions to life in prison. There were the quiet ones who usually hid in a corner or on a bunk, with a book supplied by the prison library. And there were the talkative Amsterdammers who always had a good story or joke to share. One prisoner had a good voice, and in the evening he softly and wistfully sang songs of love or of a future free from oppression.

Curiously, the days passed swiftly. We got a bread-and-water breakfast and a daily airing of ten minutes, then at noon the main meal, which alternated between stew and "blue William," the nickname for a concoction of a watery gruel of grits. Throughout the day, however, we lived with the fear of interrogation by the Gestapo or unexpected cell inspection and harassment by the guards. Evening was the most peaceful time when we had at least some privacy. But they were also the most lonely hours when I yearned for freedom and for my loved ones.

Every other Friday afternoon the Dutch Red Cross brought each prisoner a brown paper bag containing slices of nutritious wheat or rye bread, cheese or butter, perhaps, sugar, chocolate or other sweets, and cigarettes. If the Gestapo didn't withhold them as punishment for some trivial offense, the packages were the highlights of my stay in that prison and did wonders for our morale. Many times I blessed the Red Cross for that invaluable and visible signal of hope.

Early one morning toward the end of March, I heard the usual noise on the gangways, doors being opened and shut, names and commands being shouted. But this time I also heard my name: "Poley? *Mitkommen!*" I had little time for farewell. I grabbed my gear and lined up with others outside our cells. I was being transferred, but where to? Soon the whispered word passed down our ranks: "Amersfoort," and when I heard this I fell silent, scared.

Amersfoort, a transit camp where the Gestapo housed male prisoners, had become an infamous name in the Netherlands. It stood for atrocities and starvation, and it was my next destination. I had heard stories and rumors about Amersfoort.

The cruel treatment of the prisoners by the SS commanders had made the camp notorious. Deprived of freedom of action or expression, many of the underfed and the weak had broken under the viciousness of the guards. I had heard about men made to stand at attention long and excruciating hours in all sorts of weather. Or they were forced to crawl on their belly while guards jumped on their back and flailed away at them with the butt of a rifle. Those punished for camp offenses, escapees, and those sentenced to death, I had heard, endured solitary confinement in the "Bunker."

So outside the prison that morning, as we marched under heavy guard to the station and onto a train, the sunny skies contrasted with my fears. I was prepared for such a transfer, and I had written two short letters, one to my family and one to my sweetheart. When the train slowed at a road crossing, I managed to throw them out the window, praying as I did that someone would find them and forward them to the addresses indicated. They were indeed found, I learned later, and sent on. Mies still treasures hers.

At Amersfoort we marched off the station, crossed the main road from Utrecht, and turned into Laan 1914, where I caught the first glimpse of the hell-hole in which I would spend many months. Our group halted in front of the gate, and I could see the high double barbed-wire fence, the watchtowers with guards and machine guns, the searchlights, and the guards' patroling dogs. It was a menacing and frightening view.

"Johannes Poley!" a guard snapped out. I stepped forward and he shoved a strip of cloth with a number on it into my hand. It was the last time the guards used my name. From then on I was number 9238. I didn't know it at the time, but this combination of numbers would be engraved on my soul for the rest of my life. At the clothes warehouse I stripped and gave up all my possessions. Then, besides a jacket, an old pair of military trousers, and some underwear, I received the red trimmings that indicated I was a political prisoner. Wooden shoes and mess gear completed my outfit, and I was given curt instructions: "Shave yourself clean, all over, quickly. And sew those numbers onto your clothes, immediately."

It was a depressed group of men who moved towards block X. Harsh commands and foul words followed every move we made: *Schnell! Schnell!* Quickly! Quickly! Everywhere we went camp police, called *Kapos*, guarded us. They were prisoners like us but were armed with wooden sticks to keep the other prisoners in line, and we felt they had sold their souls to the devil.

We stumbled along in our wooden shoes, trying to hold on to our gear and keep our trousers from slipping down to our ankles. Inside, I secured an upper bunk that I hoped would offer some privacy in the evening hours. The first real test came during evening roll-call at 6:30. Guided by experienced prisoners, we blended into straight rows and columns and survived the head count. I managed to escape the beatings of the camp police, except for one whack which left me with a sore upper right arm.

Surprisingly the food turned out to be acceptable, although hardly sufficient. I withdrew to my bunk as soon as possible, deeply grateful to the Lord who had thus far sustained me, and fell asleep during my evening prayer.

The camp at the time included ten tar-coated wooden barracks, two sick bays, repair shops, a forge, and sheds for peeling potatoes or chopping wood. Each of the prisoners' barracks held some 600 prisoners. One group of prisoners was waiting for transportation to forced-labor camps in Germany. A smaller group of so-called political prisoners was waiting for sentencing by the Gestapo court in nearby Utrecht or for transportation to other concentration camps.

On workdays the first group was marched off to town where they worked under armed guard for local Dutch factories. It was a compromise: in return for fairly easy labor, they received good food at lunch and a comfortable place during the day.

The second group remained inside the barbed-wire fences to do menial work—clean the barracks, work in the repair shops, etc. This group, of which I was a part, wore a large red circle on the back of their jacket and on the right leg of their trousers. Several of these men had been in the camp for a long time already. Where possible, prisoners were used for work for which they qualified—serving as physician, dentist, barber, tailor, for example.

Of all that I grew to fear in that camp, Kotälla, an SS deputy commander, was the worst. He was the very devil himself, and he vented his rage on us with vulgar invectives. His moods were unpredictable and his ferocious actions were infamous. His nickname was "the executioner of Amersfoort," and his trademark was a kick in the crotch with his boot. I held my breath when I saw Kotälla with his dogs coming through the gate to take roll call, and I wondered what mood he was in. As he strutted in front of the rows of prisoners, we jumped to attention:

Achtung! Attention!

Hätlinge, Die Augen, links! Prisoners, eyes left!

Mütze, ab! Caps off!

Augen gerade, aus! Eyes front!

Abzählen! Count!

The tension rose while his subordinates walked among us, counting and probing for irregularities, and we all breathed a sign of relief when the numbers tallied and they reported back to Kotälla, satisfied.

Apart from hunger, harassment, and exhaustion, it's amazing how we lived. Every day the sickly smell of laundry cooking on the stove (not just to clean it, but also to kill the lice) filled my nostrils. On Friday night the Red Cross delivered packages of food, and on Saturday morning the latrines stunk from the vomit and feces of those who ate too much and too fast. A few hours later came the pungent odor of Lysol as the barracks' staff cleaned up the mess.

Petty thievery—a slice of bread saved for tomorrow or some cigarettes saved for bartering—was commonplace, yet degrading and frustrating. The unnerving sound of the firing squad might greet us at dawn, and often we stood for hours in the "rose garden," a barbed-wire enclosed area, when something displeased the SS officers.

In sharp contrast to the scenes of misery, I remember one clear spring morning as we stood motionless for roll call. We heard no sound except for the movement of the SS guards, counting under their breath. Then, suddenly, a caroling lark took off from the surrounding woods into the sky, and its unrestrained cheer swept over the two thousand prisoners in the square. No one dared to look for it, let alone follow it on its freedom ride. But we all heard it and took it as a symbol of liberation and light.

One evening I felt a tap on my shoulder and turned to recognized an elderly prisoner from my barracks. Eshuis was a church elder from Kampen, and several of us had gathered on his upper bunk in the corner for evening prayers during the first weeks. "I heard you're an assistant minister," he said. I confirmed it, and he told me, "Then you must lead us in our Easter worship." I was stunned, but I accepted the challenge in order to maintain my cover story. Fortunately, I had attended our pastor's confirmation class and had memorized the catechism and the supporting parts of Scripture.

So that Easter morning, behind the barbed wires of a concentration camp, I led a clandestine worship service of a small group of prisoners, and together we celebrated the victory of our Savior and God over death and the grave.

Unexpectedly one day a runner from the camp administration brought an order for me to report for interrogation. The old fears flared up again. Was my case not closed after all? When I reported to the administration, I learned that *Obersturmbann-Führer* Prof. Nelis, the SD High Commander for Religious Affairs, wanted to interrogate me.

An SS guard took me to an office building, and with clicking of boots and a "Heil Hitler," he ushered me into a large room where a strongly built man sat behind a desk. "Come in, sit down," he said as he pointed to a chair. I tried to make as little noise as possible with my wooden shoes as I headed toward the chair.

"You are Poley, assistant minister of the Dutch Reformed church in Haarlem," he stated, referring to a file in front of him. "Tell me, how did you get involved in this mess?" he asked, rather kindly.

I immediately thought of the many warnings of my resistance friends about the so-called friendly approach of the Gestapo. So I tried to choose my words carefully.

Incredibly, his kindness and interest appeared to be genuine. When I stuck to the story he must have already read from my file, he began to ask about my theological education. I threw in a remark about the many differences on theological issues between professors, how those issues at present were dividing the Dutch Reformed congregations, and how the occupying regime would certainly welcome the divisiveness.

To my great relief, he picked up the lead and began a long monologue on how Christians should obey God as their Ruler in matters of faith and church and obey the government in societal matters. After all,

173

God expressed his will in society through the government, he told me, even through an occupying force like the Romans. Didn't even St. Paul accept that?

I was amazed at his intimate knowledge of the matter, but I had heard this argument often enough to let it pass. "Your silence tells me you don't agree with me," he finally remarked, smiling. "But when all this messy war business is over, you'll be amazed at the great society we will build together."

His confidence that we would both be around to enjoy that future was reassuring and amusing at the same time. He closed the file and I jumped to attention again. He called the guard and dismissed me with a few noncommittal words. With a silent prayer of thanks in my heart, I breathed a huge sigh of relief as I entered the camp gate again.

After a few days at Amersfoort, to my surprise, I experienced less random cruelty and better food than I had expected. Later I learned that the Dutch commander of the Red Cross in Amersfoort, Mrs. Loes van Overeem, had achieved a sort of truce with the SS commander of the camp. She was a fairly young lady, known to the prisoners as, "the Angel of Amersfoort." She had demanded regular inspections of the camp and its hygiene, as well as personal access to the prisoners and to the sick-bay, etc. She cajoled, threatened, and blackmailed the SS commanders so effectively that they apparently decided to give in to her demands.

Every Friday afternoon she personally accompanied the trucks with the food packages, and we saw her chatting amiably with the SS officers, meanwhile making sure all the packages were distributed among the prisoners and not to the guards. She also talked with the prisoners in charge of the camp to get inside information directly, and this resulted, at least for the time being, in more humane treatment.

We still endured the brutal beatings and punishments and the long, exhausting hours of standing to attention. The unpredictable executions continued, but the extreme violence and starvation that made life so unbearable disappeared.

I quickly learned to make myself inconspicuous and to avoid most of the beatings. Then I was given an unexpected opportunity. The prisoner who acted as administrator of our barrack became ill with pneumonia and was taken to the sickbay for an extended stay. It resulted in chaos during the roll call that night, and it took several hours to convince the SS guards that the total number of prisoners tallied with their numbers for our block.

After the "all clear," most of the prisoners turned in to make the most of the few hours remaining till dawn, but I made my way to the *Block-Älteste,* the prisoner in charge of our barrack. He was responsible for its cleanliness, for order, and for the strict observance of the SS directives. The chaos the evening before had left him desperate, so when I volunteered to take on the job of barracks administrator, he jumped at the offer. Within a day Block X had a clean administrative slate again and managed to stay out of that kind of trouble from then on. It was a demanding job, but relatively comfortable. I made a few good friends in both the barracks and camp staff, and in a concentration camp nothing beats the comfort given by good friends. This made it easier to cope with the daily harassment and cruelties of the SS guards.

One chilly afternoon I registered a large number of new prisoners to replace those who had left earlier that day. When his turn came, a shivering, fragile man in badly fitting camp clothes moved uneasily to my table. I recognized him immediately. He was Dr. J. van der Elst, the amiable principal of the high school I had attended and where I had taken my university admission exams. Like all prisoners I was shaved bald, and he didn't recognize me until I introduced myself. Seven years before he had registered me as his high school student. Now I was returning the compliment and sorry to be doing it. He was the last person I expected to see in a concentration camp. As principal he had had the responsibility of keeping the school operating and out of trouble, and he went out of his way to achieve that. He regularly censored the school paper and the recitation competitions, forbidding texts or poems he thought would provoke the Nazis. He stopped any activity that might attract their attention and bring on measures that would jeopardize the school. We young people, who yet had few responsibilities, thought he went much too far.

Why in the world would this cautious man be arrested? I wondered. I registered him and later that afternoon tried to make him as comfortable as possible under the miserable circumstances. That evening, when he was able to calm down a bit, he told me the story. Some days before, Gestapo agents came to the school and demanded the names and addresses of the boys who would leave the school in a few weeks after final exams. Dr. van der Elst knew the list would be used to deport the boys to Germany to forced-labor camps, so he flatly refused. The Gestapo arrested him on the spot, along with the chairman of the school board, and sent them both to concentration camp.

The moment of truth had come to this overcautious and prudent administrator, the choice to give in and bow to the enemy or to stand up to them and refuse. He stood up for his convictions and accepted the consequences. And here he was, a shivering and tiny man, yet so large and courageous.

I hadn't been there very long when a tall, robust prisoner stopped me in the sandy corridor between the barracks. "They tell me that you are Poley from Haarlem. I am Schaapman from the Haarlem police headquarters. We're in this together."

I was shocked. "What happened," I asked him. "How come they arrested you? I didn't mention any police contacts in my story."

"I'll tell you all about it after the evening meal," he said softly.

Later he told me he had been on duty that night and had secretly contacted Mrs. van Asch. She asked him to find a way to warn van Rijn of his impending arrest. When the Gestapo called on him that Saturday evening after van Rijn and I were arrested, they told him denial wouldn't help, that Mrs van Asch had confessed to asking him, and that I had confessed to receiving a note at the Lakenkoopersstraat address.

After hearing this, he realized it was probably the

least damaging way out of the mess, and the ten Boom connection wouldn't surface that way. So he admitted his alleged part in it. Schaapman was quite matter-of-fact about it all, accepting what happened as a calculated risk gone wrong. I hardly knew what to say. I was highly embarrassed and grateful at the same time.

It was the first of many get-togethers during which we got to know each other quite well. He was quite a bit older than I and became a sort of father figure to me as well as friend. As a barracks administrator I had sufficient food, and I could give him my Red Cross cigarettes to exchange for extra food. When our *Block-Älteste* (the prisoner in charge of other prisoners) was unexpectedly included in a prisoners' transport, I told the *Lager-Älteste* (the prisoner in charge of the entire camp,) that Schaapman was a police officer who might qualify to become our new *Block-Älteste*. He took the suggestion, and from then on Schaapman ruled Block X with a fair but strict rule. As his barracks administrator, I slept in the same corner and, with my frequent trips to the camp administration, I could pass on advance warnings of suspicious SS activity, which usually meant unscheduled inspections or roll calls.

(After my release I took a letter from Schaapman to his wife in Haarlem, along with a charcoal portrait of him, sketched by a fellow prisoner. She was deeply moved. Even under the sad circumstances I could cheer her up with the news that he was doing quite well and he was optimistic about his future. After the war, however, I learned that Schaapman didn't survive. He was sent to a concentration camp in northern Germany and was finally liberated, but unfortunately he died in a British field hospital from the hardships he experienced.)

In mid-July of 1944, I was asked to join the *Schreibstube,* the camp administration, where they kept an accurate and up-to-date record of the movement and count of all the prisoners in the camp. The *Lager-Älteste,* Frans van de Laar, operated from there. He had the awesome responsibility of representing all the prisoners to the SS commanders. A mistake by him, such as an incorrect report on roll call numbers or a remark or behavior that displeased the SS staff could carry severe punishment for thousands of prisoners. But he was also our intermediary and often the intercessor on behalf of the prisoners. So he had to remain in good standing with the camp commanders. By maintaining a severe but just discipline, he somehow managed to walk that tightrope successfully.

In the camp administration, we had to provide him, almost hourly, with exact information on the numbers of prisoners and their whereabouts, and we could do that only by meticulously keeping our own lists and by a daily check with the barrack numbers. These served as the basis for the barracks' totals at roll call and for provision of food rations, Red Cross packages, etc.

My "promotion" to deputy camp administrator brought definite advantages. The administration was a kind of halfway house for SS staff. They stopped by frequently to announce unexpected roll calls or transports or to pass on new orders or lists of prisoners coming in or leaving, and they often brought visitors they wanted to impress. For them, the camp administration served as a model of a well-run camp, and that included the prisoners who worked there.

For me it meant decent military clothes and shoes and permission to let my hair grow into a crew-cut. Although offered a bunk close by, I chose—with permission of both the *Lager-Älteste* and *Block-Älteste*—to keep the quarters in my old barrack. My friends were there, and I could share the news and miseries of the day each evening with them.

While working in the administration office one day I intercepted a list of prisoners scheduled for transport to a forced-labor camp in Germany. As I scanned it, I stopped, shocked, and went over it again. There it was: *Poley, number 9238.* There was no further information and no reasons were given. Apparently I had served my time. But Nazi Germany definitely was not in my plans for my life. As soon as possible I excused myself and went to the doctor's offices. A friend, Dr. Kooistra, was on duty, and I told him about my problem. "Report to sick-parade for doctor's check tomorrow morning," he ordered with a smile.

The next morning he had a small form filled out and ready for a signature by the head camp doctor, claiming that I was diagnosed with tuberculosis. It was well-known that such patients were not welcome in Germany, and this information would, like everything else, find its way into the SS files.

A few weeks later, on August 15, I received a list of prisoners to be released the next day, and there it was again: Poley, number 9238. I stared at it and read it over and over through clouded eyes. And so on August 16, six months after I was arrested, I walked out of the gates of the concentration camp. In civilian clothes and carrying many letters and messages for the families of the friends I had made in this place, I headed for freedom.

Many of the bad experiences of those months have faded with the years, but the good memories remain: the shared feelings, the mutual despair and hope, the comfort and help, the joint efforts to minimize the damage done by the SS.

Above and beyond all human comfort, however, was the continuing presence of my Father in heaven sustaining me. That inner peace made me invulnerable to the constant abuse by the forces of evil.

THEIR DARKEST WINTER;
THEIR SWEETEST MAY
14

I came home to a jubilant and deeply grateful circle of family and friends for whom my release came as a complete surprise. Mies had been staying with relatives on an island south of Rotterdam, and she was soon on her way to Haarlem. Throughout my imprisonment, Mies and my parents had shared their anguish. My parents had realized how serious our love had become, and Mies had become quite close to them.

I couldn't go outside anymore without running a great risk, so my father went to meet her at the ferry in Rotterdam and proudly escorted her home. And there, after so many months of fear and agony, were her blue eyes and outstretched arms. It was the moment I had yearned for so intensely, and I couldn't get enough of it. We couldn't let go of each other. We walked hand in hand through the house or sat on the couch, my arm around her. Only then was my freedom complete.

We told stories of what and how things had happened, and how we had longed for signs of life of one another, but I didn't share the details of the hunger, the misery, the evils of prison camp with anyone. It wouldn't serve any purpose, and it would spoil the joy of our reunion. Instead we talked about the future, as uncertain as that was, and made our plans. We learned about Opa's death, and that saddened us, but we learned to be grateful for every new day we had together.

Later I realized I had narrowly escaped a terrible fate. In early September the Allied forces broke through in the North, causing an enormous upheaval in the western Netherlands. German troops moved east, and many Nazi supporters and functionaries fled. The Gestapo rounded up thousands of prisoners from the Dutch concentration camps in Vught and Amersfoort and transported them to camps further east and north in Germany. Many of my camp friends were deported, only to die of deprivation.

The advancing armies also left Mies stranded in Haarlem, cutting her off from her family in Zeeland, who were liberated shortly afterward. We found some of Mary's dresses that had been hidden in my parents' home, and, fortunately, she could wear those. And she was able to temporarily attend a nearby teacher's college.

Several days later, General Montgomery launched his abortive push for Arnhem, the operation called

"Market Garden," and described in the book and the movie *A Bridge Too Far*. The Dutch railroad workers then went on strike to support the Allied offensive. Thus the western part of our country, known as Holland, was effectively cut off from its resources. It had to struggle on its own through what became the darkest winter in Dutch history. Food and fuel were scarce. The bitter cold took a terrible toll, especially in the cities, and thousands died. We survived on tulip bulbs and beans, and we gathered twigs and dry wood to burn for heat.

Even under desperate circumstances, the resistance work continued, encouraged by the Allied advances, and developed into full-scale guerilla war. At that age, if I were out on the streets I would be arrested on sight, but my father was heavily involved.

The Gestapo was unrelenting in its manhunts, arresting hundreds of resistance workers and shooting many immediately. Our friend Piet Hartog, for example, Aty van Woerden's fiancé, died this way. He had visited the BéJé often and worked in a military intelligence group called the *Rolls Royce*. He was arrested with a co-worker and in his letter from prison he wrote about his faith in Christ in the face of death. He was shot, without a trial, on January 30, 1945.

The resistance fought back, however. Early one morning in October I heard a lot of noise in the street, and we learned that a Dutch Gestapo officer had been shot on the Westergracht, only about 1,000 feet from our home. The Germans were combing the

neighborhood for evidence of the underground execu-
tioners.

Quickly we hid everything incriminating and
watched for unwanted visitors, but no search parties
came to our street. Later in the day we heard commotion again and saw people pointing in the direction of
the Westergracht. From the windows of our top floor
we soon saw heavy billows of smoke. Unable to find
the culprits who shot the Gestapo officer, they set fire
to several houses.

In the middle of winter an elderly Jewish lady who
was hiding in our home died, apparently of a heart
attack. My mother found her on the floor of the bedroom she shared with Mies, and we were suddenly
faced with the problem of burial. Officially, she didn't
exist, and we couldn't get a burial permit until she
was illegally entered into the city records with a false
identity. That took ten days, during which time our
home remained her hiding place. Fortunately it was
very cold at the time. With the help of a trustworthy
physician and an undertaker, we were able to pro-
ceed. After much searching, we even located one of
the woman's relatives in time for the burial.

Early on Sunday morning, March 15, the Gestapo,
aided by German army patrols, cracked down on the
L.O. resistance network in Haarlem in a simultaneous raid on many addresses, including my home. I
managed to hide in time under the living room floor
through a hidden hatch, while my brother hid all
signs of my presence in our bedroom. They were after
my father, and they beat him and forcefully interro-

gated him. Apparently he managed a convincing performance of a weak, innocent, and scared old man, because they soon left him and went on to their next address. They arrested many others in Haarlem, however, on that black Sunday, and they shot several of them in the following weeks. We survived but lost several friends and brothers-in-arms.

In the midst of this turmoil Corrie ten Boom, Tante Kees, came home to a starved city and a cold and ransacked home that had been sealed by the Gestapo. Only with difficulty could the house be opened up again. Even then, it was a tragic homecoming, without the love and warmth of her father and sister, and an unending emptiness. But there was the vision! During their imprisonment, Betsie and Corrie had had a vision in which they would be aiding war victims right after their liberation. It was that vision that inspired Corrie and gave her the courage to start anew.

With Corrie back, the BéJé was accessible again. We met with her several times that winter. Mies retrieved some of Tante Martha's clothes which, by some miracle, hadn't been stolen. Once, when Tante Kees visited us in March, she told us that she still woke up every night around roll call time. She smiled and said that she made the most of these early-morning hours putting to paper her memories. She had started her book *Gevangene, en toch . . . (Prisoner, and yet . . .).*

As the winter months dragged on, the situation in Holland became desperate, attracting the attention of the world. The Swedish Red Cross negotiated with the German authorities for permission to ship in flour and butter, and we shall never forget the whiteness and the taste of the loaves that were distributed.

Finally, toward the end of April, with the Allied armies advancing on Berlin, the International Red Cross persuaded the Germans to allow a fleet of Allied bombers to drop food. The antiaircraft guns remained silent while Operation Mannah, as it was called, brought food from heaven.

A few days later came the sweetest May in our history: the occupying German army in Holland unconditionally surrendered. After five years and several hundred thousand deaths, we were free again.

We had saved our red, white, and blue flags for this occasion, and they flew from almost every house. But in spite of the unconditional surrender and the flags waving, liberation was slow to arrive. For several days we lived in a no man's land between slavery and deliverance, uncertain of the reaction of the still present German army units.

Then finally! Finally! On Tuesday, May 8, the victorious Canadian armored cars and tanks rolled into Haarlem. They were surrounded by thousands of jubilant and flag-waving Dutch, hugging and shouting. Imprisoned resistance workers were set free, church bells tolled to proclaim the newfound life, and prayers were said for those still in captivity in the East. Sadly, many would never return.

Mies and I joined the crowd and made our way downtown to witness the hand over of power. The main streets were crowded with rejoicing residents and we had to go through back roads. Skirting the old St. Bavo

Church via Smedestraat, we came to the BéJé where Tante Kees was arranging a memorial to Grandfather in the shop window. She placed the large painting of him directly behind the Bible which was open at Psalm 91. And she had arranged several smaller pictures and some of his personal possessions and decorated them with orange ribbon. It was a moving tribute to one who gave his life so that others might live.

She embraced us effusively. After going through so much trouble and sorrow together, it seemed fitting that the three of us rejoice together for our freedom. We parked our bikes in the narrow corridor and walked on to the town square to converge with the elated crowd and into a new life of freedom.

THE WAY OF RECONCILIATION 15

Those of us who survived the war tried to return to a normal life as soon as possible. We had to lay aside the weapons we had learned to use in the battle against evil; lying, stealing, and cheating could have no place in our lives anymore. Searching and stumbling, sometimes falling, getting up and trying again, we had to find ways to make righteousness reign in our own lives. I returned to Delft Technological University and received my degree as a physicist.

Mies and I were married and we settled in Wassenaar and began to raise a family. Over the years we met several times with Tante Kees, or Corrie ten Boom, as she was called after the war, in Haarlem or at her home in Overveen.

Corrie's dramatic healing came in 1947. She had gone to Germany with a message of God's forgiveness. At a church in Munich she recognized one of her former guards from the prison camp, Ravensbrück, and all the horror of those months came rushing back. She saw the visored cap with its skull and crossbones, the leather riding crop hanging from the belt, and the shiny black boots. And she remembered the shame of having to walk past this man, naked, under the harsh glare of lights.

After the meeting he approached her, hand extended, and, to Corrie's utter amazement, asked, "Fraulein, will you forgive me for what I did?" He had become a Christian since the war and had asked forgiveness from God. He didn't remember Corrie personally, but she represented all those he had treated so miserably, and he wanted to receive forgiveness from one of them. "I stood there with the coldness clutching my heart," Corrie recalled, "unable to lift my hand." Finally, mechanically, at what she later believed was the prompting of the Spirit of God, she thrust her hand into his, and God's forgiveness flowed through her to her former captor.

Unlike Corrie, I was not faced with the problem of personal forgiveness. I didn't feel hatred toward any one of those who had mistreated me. I had joined the resistance knowing full well the risks. Those who arrested me had nothing against me personally. Whatever abuse I received, I felt came impersonally from the Gestapo, the SS, or the *Kapos,* Dutch prisoners working for the Germans. I loathed them as a group, but I put no specific face to it.

I felt this same general hatred toward all Germans. They had occupied and ravaged my country. They had murdered innocent Jewish citizens as well as my friends who stood for righteousness. In that first flush of freedom I could not distinguish between Nazis and Germans. I had seen too many German soldiers assisting the Gestapo, the hated and much-feared security police, in their dirty work, and the distinction escaped me.

Many Christians told me that it was my Christian duty to forgive the Germans, collectively, but to me that was—and still is—well-meant nonsense. The Bible teaches human forgiveness only between individuals—and after repentance. Moreover, even to think about forgiving the Nazis their atrocities would be to trespass arrogantly into a realm that was sacred to my Jewish friends. As far as I was concerned, I was through with the Germans, their language, and their country, for the rest of my life. I thoroughly hated all of it.

As a university student I took part in the Dutch chapter of the Intervarsity Fellowship of Evangelical Students. Each summer the group held a convention in Lunteren, and representatives from other countries attended. In the summer of 1948, the German chapter of the IFES wrote and asked to be allowed to send representatives.

After long, impassioned discussions and personal soul searching, we unanimously agreed to let them come. When the German delegation arrived, however, we sat down with them and explained our reservations. Yes, we were one in Christ, but an abyss of crimes and bad feelings still separated many of us.

Surprisingly, they told us they had expected this,

193

but they came anyway, and they wanted us to know how deeply they regretted their part in the war and their silence in the face of a demonic regime.

This made me very uneasy. I had heard such confessions and regrets after the war all too often from German-friendly Dutch. But for the few days of that convention I determined to push those feelings aside. So we prayed together for God's guidance, then began the meetings.

I stayed close to one of the leaders, a student named Hans Kombächer. Something about him told me it would be important. We prayed in small groups, shared together in Bible studies, and praised God while singing. But I was still uncomfortable. I didn't hate Hans at all. On the contrary, I began to see him as a brother in Christ, as needy as I was, honest and searching. I had nothing to forgive him for. He had done nothing to me. Still, I felt a deep hatred for Germany and for Germans for all they had done. Yet in my heart I knew that hate doesn't heal.

It was a message in one of the Bible studies that the Lord used to point out the way to me. The speaker read a verse from II Corinthians: "God, Who reconciled us to Himself through Christ, gave us the ministry of reconciliation."

Reconciliation! There was my answer. I had to go beyond just forgiving. I had to begin a new relationship. God has reconciled us to himself in Christ. And if He begins with us anew, shouldn't we begin anew with our brothers and neighbors if they repent? Suddenly I was at peace. I knew what I had to do.

That didn't take all the bumps out of the road, of course, nor make the journey without hazards. But the intense hate, the anger, and the bitterness were

194

gone. I learned to identify the Nazis and their regime as the origin of the atrocities. I learned to listen to and to trust and accept acknowledgments of guilt and responsibility from Niemöller and from such great German statesmen as Willy Brandt and Richard von Weiszäcker. And I tried earnestly not to pass my own feelings on to the next generation.

Old feelings die hard, however. I still cringe at the color combination of red and black, (the uniform colors of the Dutch-collaborating National Socialitsche Beweging), at the sound of marching boots and shouted commands in German, and at the playing of the German national anthem, *Deutschland, Deutschland über Alles.* "Germany above all" it means, and it still makes me shiver. Hunger still makes me irritable and unreasonable.

I still keep Germans, their language, and their country at arm's length. It is, no doubt, a defense mechanism born out of those years of suffering, and, perhaps, I'll never get it out of my system. But now I make a new beginning with each German I meet. I'm not a captive of hate anymore. I have found a new way—the way of reconciliation.

THE HIDING PLACE
REVISITED
16

Through *The Hiding Place*, the world now knows what happened to Corrie and Betsie ten Boom in prison and then in concentration camp. Corrie gave the most authentic account in her memoirs, *Gevangene en Toch. . .* and in her collection *Prison Letters,* published in 1975.

The two women were confined in prison in Scheveningen from February 29 to June 5, 1944. Betsie was put in cell 314 and Corrie in cell 384 in solitary confinement on March 16, after first being in a cell with four others. They were interrogated there by the Gestapo but not mistreated.

While at Scheveningen, the ten Boom sisters took all the guilt upon themselves and thus exonerated the others arrested with them. They never betrayed those to whom they offered shelter, nor did they mention any names. In prison they learned of their father's death, and they heard of the escape of the six in the hiding place—the Angels' Den—in the BéJé.

From the first moment of the ordeal, Betsie made a better spiritual adjustment to prison life than Corrie. "Physically and spiritually," she wrote, "I feel well. My soul is very peaceful."

Corrie had more difficulty finding that quiet and peace, but later, in solitary confinement, she wrote about her rediscovered trust: "I talk to my Savior . . . I am no longer alone. God is with me."

On D-day, June 6, 1944, they were sent to the Dutch concentration camp in Vught near Hertogenbosch and brought together again: Betsie, number 01130, and Corrie, number 01131. As Corrie wrote, "We can accept it, we are in God's training school." Then in early September they were taken to Germany and imprisoned in Ravensbrück concentration camp. Betsie died there on December 14, 1944, from chronic illness, exhaustion, starvation, and hardship. On December 28, 1944, Corrie was unexpectedly released through an administrative error.

After the war, Corrie searched for the right way to serve God. Convinced that she had been released for a specific purpose, she spent several years caring for victims of the war and for displaced persons.

But more and more she turned to directly telling people about God. She discovered that people hungered to hear the ten Boom story of spiritual survival. Her message, "Jesus saves, even in deepest Nazi hell," became her liberating theme for countless meetings in countries all over the world. Assisted by several secretaries, she travelled the globe and became the well-known "Tramp for the Lord," a cheerful missionary for her Savior. And the success of her book and the movie made of it, made her a household name in Christian circles around the world.

In the summer of 1978, Corrie suffered a stroke and died peacefully on April 15, 1983. She is now with her father and sister—part of that great cloud of witnesses of faith that surrounds us and cheers us on.

In a television interview toward the end of Corrie's life, the interviewer observed, "You must have a mighty great faith." She answered by quoting her beloved father: "I do not have a mighty great faith, but I have faith in a mighty great God."

Remarkably enough, in the light of the horrors we experienced together, the survivors of the BéJé had little contact after the war. We each had our own grief to overcome and own losses of family, friends, and homes, as well as years of our lives, to deal with. We each struggled to gain a new perspective on life and to find the courage to build anew. Neither our starved and impoverished nation nor our devastated culture had the resources or structures to help. Some in our community could not even find a shoulder to weep on.

Those arrested with the ten Booms on that fateful afternoon survived their imprisonment. The Gestapo raided the BéJé because it was an underground shelter for Jews. There is no indication they had evidence of other types of resistance work by the ten Booms. Their goals achieved, and with no direct evidence against any of the others, the Gestapo gradually released them.

* * * * * * * * *

Leendert Kip continued his career, at first as a teacher in mathematics. Later, he was one of the happy few who made his hobby into a living, teaching his beloved Dutch language and literature. At first he taught at the *Dreefschool,* then at a teachers' college in Bloemendaal, near Haarlem.

* * * * * * * *

Mirjam de Jong was one of the few of her family to survive. Mies and I met with her and Henk Wiedijk during the summer of 1945, but lost contact with both of them shortly after. Mirjam left the Netherlands to become an early Jewish settler in pre-Israel Palestine where she survived four more wars—1948, 1957, 1967, and 1973.

* * * * * * * *

Both Paula and Meta Monsanto (Tante Martha) survived. They remained good friends of my parents while reestablishing their lives in the Hague. Both worked in government offices, Paula as a rebellious maverick on a motorbike and Meta as a quiet and wise lady, both very hospitable and very energetic. When Mies and I were married, we settled quite close to the Hague, and their friendship greatly enriched our family life for many years until they died.

* * * * * * * *

I lost track of Thea, Hansje Frankfort-Israels, but I

know that her husband didn't survive the war.

* * * * * * * *

Mary was liberated from the Angels' Den only to be arrested at her new hiding place. Against all instructions and training, she fell for the manipulative sweet talk of the Gestapo officer and mentioned the names of several persons who "should be warned." As a result, several were arrested, including Jan Vermeer and the Minnema family.

Mary was deported via Vught to the women's concentration camp in Theresienstadt where she died. When her parents took their own lives to escape Nazi persecution, her sophisticated world fell apart. An instinctive hope and will to live kept her going for a while, but the filth, cruelty, and deprivation of the concentration camp finished her.

To have known her so well was a privilege, and to lose her was a deep personal loss. I'll never forget her singing *Solveig's Lied*. When we heard the sad news some time after the war, Eusi said, and we all agreed, "May her memory be a blessing."

* * * * * * * *

Eusi survived, but barely. He was arrested in April, 1945, at his hiding place in Sneek, Friesland. By that time the Allied armies had already penetrated so deeply into Germany that transportation of any prisoners towards the East was out of the question. Liberation came to him in his cell at the police station. Miraculously, all his family members survived, and he was reunited with them. Mies and I had difficulty

A page from the guestbook of the BéJé,
March 6, 1974

Bellaart 6.'74.

vandaag na 30 jaren geleden, toen ik hier
ondergedoken was, hier geweest! Bij de schuilplaats,
heb ik een lofzegging gesproken die ik verder
in mijn leven nog niet eerder uitgesproken
had. en wel deze! "Geloofd zijt Gij Eeuwige
onze God, Koning van de wereld, die aan
mij een wonder gedaan heeft op deze plaats"

Eusi

Mary werd een paar dagen later gepakt
Haars aandenken zij ten zegen.

Hans   Eusi

                        D. Hossel Roos

Ps. 66 : 10 - 14 onberijmd
- al mijn geloften Ik betalen
U, die in nood mij hebt behoed ---

                Hans Poley   BéJé mei '43 - Feb. '44

Mies Poley - Wessels   Annelie Poley

A page from the guestbook of the BéJé,
March 6, 1974

English Translation

March 6, 1974

Today, 30 years after I was hiding here, I was here
again. At this Hiding Place I said a special doxology
that I have never said before: "Praise be to Thee,
Eternal, our God, King of the world, Who has done to
me a miracle at this place."

Eusi

Mary was arrested a few days later. May her memory be a blessing.

Hans   Eusi

Psalm 66:10-14   Dora Mossel-Roos

Hans Poley BéJé May '43-Feb. '44
Mies Poley-Wessels   Anneke Poley

finding him and his wife in the undescribable chaos in Amsterdam, but our meeting was unforgettable. After the war he served the decimated Jewish congregations of Amsterdam and later served in the Hague as a cantor and a teacher.

Eusi and I came to know each other so well during the seven months in hiding at the BéJé that my wife and I were two of the few Christians Eusi accepted. It is very difficult for a kosher-living Jewish family to socialize with unclean Gentiles. But in spite of Eusi's continuing distrust of Christians, our wartime friendship remained alive. To celebrate my fiftieth birthday, he planted a tree in my name in Israel.

One day early in March, 1974, we went together to the BéJé and up the well-known staircase to the upper floors. Memories and emotions overwhelmed us as we thought of those we would never see again.

After reminiscing for some time, Eusi said, "I'm going to fulfill my promise." While in the hiding place after the Gestapo raid thirty years before he had vowed to the Almighty that if he survived he would return to sing praise to the Almighty. So he went to Tante Kees' room and soon I heard that mighty voice that I had heard so often, praising the Almighty but also bewailing those we lost.

The climax of the day came when we went downstairs to find that Corrie had returned because the film of her book *The Hiding Place* was being shot. We had not seen her in many years, and she greeted me in her own disarming way: "Hans, where have your dark hairs gone?" It was an emotional reunion, one of the few occasions in which several of the survivors of the wartime BéJé met with the family.

There was so much to be said. We relived those

fateful events and remembered those who had lived in the house with us but had not survived. In the afternoon Corrie took us to the location where *The Hiding Place* was being filmed. When the actors and actresses learned who we were, they showered us with questions about the actual circumstances of those months of hiding. When we left, late in the afternoon, it was as though an unfinished chapter in Eusi's life had finally been closed. Mies and I remained Eusi's trusted friends until his death and helped to lay him to rest at Wassenaar.

My copy of Corrie's book *Gevangene en Toch . . .* carries his dedication, "The righteous of the nations will be part of the world to come."

ABOUT THE AUTHOR

After the war, Hans Poley completed his degree at Delft Technological Institute as a physicist, and later he earned his Ph.D. He and his longtime sweetheart, Mies Wessels, were married in February, 1949, and have two sons and a daughter. He has worked as research physicist for the Dutch Defense Research Council and for Royal Dutch/Shell's International Exploration and Production (E&P) Division. For a year he worked in Houston, Texas, as an exchange scientist for Shell. In 1977 he became Shell's Advisor for E&P Safety and Environmental Affairs until he retired in 1984. He was awarded the Dutch Resistance Memorial Cross for the work he did for his country during World War II.